PENGUIN B

Curry
BIBLE

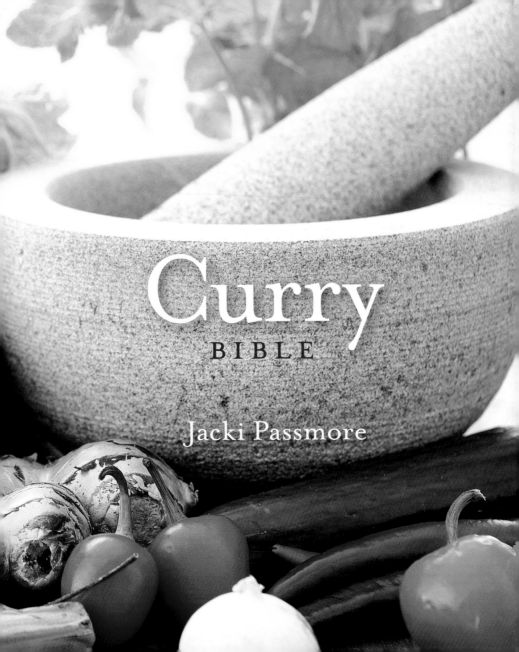

Curry

BIBLE

Jacki Passmore

Contents

Introduction

Curries in the western world have come a long way since the days when, in the average home, they largely consisted of a stew of meat, and sometimes fruit such as sultanas, flavoured with bought English 'curry powder', a legacy of British colonialists in India. A staple food of most Asia-Pacific cuisines, with innumerable regional variations, curries have been (and continue to be) adopted and adapted all around the world, to suit local ingredients and tastes.

In this book you'll find 140 inspiring, irresistible recipes for curry dishes from regional India and Pakistan, Burma and Thailand, Singapore and Sri Lanka, Indonesia and Malaysia. There are practical tips on buying, preparing and storing spices and pastes; stocking the pantry; preparing traditional accompaniments such as rice and sambals; and producing fast curries without sacrificing flavour.

Curry basics

A curry is essentially a dish flavoured with dried and fresh spices and cooked in a sauce based on onions, garlic and ginger. Curries are not always hot. In India, Thailand, South Asia and Malaysia, for example, the emphasis is typically on achieving aroma and flavour through the careful blending of spices, which are usually ground just before use. The most common spices used are chilli, coriander, cumin, and turmeric, but the range is enormous, usually based on regional tastes. Including yoghurt or coconut milk in the dish makes for a milder result.

You don't need any special kitchen equipment to make curries: you can cook them in your normal pots and pans. For grinding dry spices, a mortar and pestle, a blender or an electric coffee grinder are invaluable. The same goes for grinding wet seasonings (e.g. onion, ginger and garlic), for which a food processor with a small bowl and metal blade also comes in very handy.

imparted, so for colour but moderate heat, add them at the last minute. Chilli paste or sauce can replace fresh chillies in some recipes.

FRESH HERBS

When selecting herbs look for bright greens, perky leaves and upstanding stems. Avoid wilted or curling specimens with browned tips or specks. In cool weather, fresh herbs can be kept in a glass of cold water. Otherwise, untie the bunch, wrap herbs in a damp paper towel, tie in a plastic bag and refrigerate for up to 5 days.

Alternatively, why not grow your own? All you need is a few pots and a sunny spot . . . The most common curry herbs are basil, coriander, kaffir lime leaves, lemongrass and mint – all of which are easy to grow at home.

Staple recipes

COOKING RICE

Allow 1 cup uncooked rice per 2–3 people I usually don't wash rice before cooking, but if you do, allow slightly less water if cooking by the absorption method.

Absorption method: For 1 cup long-grain rice allow 2 cups water, and 1½ cups of water for every additional 1 cup of rice. Cover and bring to the boil, reduce heat to very low and allow to cook for 12–15 minutes untouched. Lift the lid and stir rice with a chopstick.

To boil: Bring a large saucepan of salted water to the boil, pour in rice and boil for about 12 minutes, stirring occasionally. Tip into a colander to drain.

Saffron Rice Pilaf

Cook basmati rice by your preferred method, then drain. Gently fry sultanas and chopped almonds or pistachios in a generous amount of ghee. Infuse saffron threads in a little boiling milk until golden. Stir sultanas, nuts and saffron milk through the rice just before serving.

Coconut Rice
Cook by the absorption method, substituting coconut milk or diluted coconut cream for the water, and season generously with salt, which brings out the flavour of the coconut.

Turmeric Rice
Add 1–2 teaspoons of ground turmeric to the water when boiling rice or using the absorption method. Can be used for both plain and coconut rice.

Curry accompaniments

FOR INDIAN CURRIES

- Long-grain white rice, boiled or steamed
- Indian bread
  A variety of ready-made Indian breads can be purchased
  in supermarkets or Asian stores. Heat according to
  directions.
- Raita
  Beat natural yoghurt and season with salt. Stir in any of
  the following: grated cucumber, minced shallots, chopped
  mint or coriander, mashed banana, chopped dill.
- Chutney
  For flavour contrast serve sweet and fruity chutneys
  with hot curries, hot and spicy chutneys with vegetarian
  curries and creamy or mild meat curries.
- Tomato and Cucumber Salad
  Sliced cucumber and wedges of tomato are a popular
  edible garnish for Indian curries, and help to combat

FOR INDONESIAN AND MALAYSIAN CURRIES

- Long-grain white rice, boiled or steamed; coconut rice; turmeric rice
- Crunchy garnish
  - coconut (freshly grated, or toasted desiccated or shredded coconut)
  - fried onion/garlic flakes (available from Asian stores)
  - fried ikan bilis (miniature anchovies)
- Spicy sambal (available from Asian food stores)
- Hardboiled eggs, cut in half
- Sliced cucumber

Powders and pastes

These days you can buy good-quality curry mixes in most supermarkets as well as Asian food stores. But making your own doesn't take much time or effort and it definitely gives you a fresher, more flavourful result. Pastes in particular keep well: you can store them in an airtight container (such as a small storage bag) for up to a week in the fridge or up to 1 year in the freezer.

Correct storage ensures that curry pastes and pickles retain their full flavour and do not attract mould. After using some, smooth what is left and cover with a film of oil to prevent spoiling. Again, cover tightly and refrigerate or keep in a cool part of the kitchen.

Garam masala

2 tablespoons coriander seeds

1 tablespoon cumin seeds

1 tablespoon peppercorns

4 cloves

4 cardamom pods, cracked

2-cm cinnamon stick

In a small pan without oil, roast the coriander, cumin and peppercorns over moderate heat until they are very aromatic (about 1½ minutes). Tip into a blender or spice grinder with the remaining ingredients, and grind to a fine powder. Pass through a fine sieve and allow to cool before storing in an airtight container.

MAKES ENOUGH FOR 1 CURRY

Thai red curry paste

2 tablespoons coriander seeds

1–2 teaspoons white peppercorns

2 teaspoons ground hot paprika

1½ teaspoons shrimp paste

vegetable oil

1 stalk lemongrass, chopped

6 shallots, chopped

2-cm piece fresh ginger, chopped

5 cloves garlic, chopped

4 fresh hot red chillies,
deseeded and chopped

1 teaspoon salt

Heat the coriander seeds and peppercorns in a dry nonstick pan until very aromatic (about 1½ minutes), stirring continually. Tip into a spice grinder and grind finely. Add the paprika and set mixture aside.

Cook the shrimp paste in a little vegetable oil, until pungent (about 40 seconds). Add to the spices.

Place the lemongrass, shallots, ginger, garlic, chillies and salt in a mortar, food processor or blender. Grind to a paste, adding the prepared spices and shrimp paste. Continue to grind, adding enough vegetable oil to make a smooth thick paste.

Use at once, or keep for up to 1 week in an airtight container in the refrigerator. To keep paste for a few weeks, cook in a nonstick pan with 1–2 tablespoons extra oil for 3–4 minutes, and then store.

MAKES ABOUT 1 CUP (ENOUGH FOR 2–4 CURRIES)

Thai green curry paste

2 teaspoons coriander seeds

1½ teaspoons shrimp paste

4 spring onions, chopped

4 large mild green chillies,
  deseeded and chopped

6 small hot green chillies,
  deseeded and chopped

2 stalks lemongrass, chopped

½ cup fresh coriander leaves

grated zest of 1 lime

3 cloves garlic, chopped

3-cm piece fresh ginger,
  chopped

1½ teaspoons salt

vegetable oil

Roast the coriander seeds and shrimp paste in a dry pan for 1 minute, then transfer to a mortar or spice grinder and grind to a paste.

Transfer to a blender or processor with a metal blade. Add remaining ingredients (except the oil) and grind everything together until very smooth. Continue to grind, adding enough vegetable oil to make a smooth thick paste. Pass through a sieve if necessary to remove large bits.

Use at once, or keep for up to 1 week in an airtight container in the refrigerator. To keep paste for a few weeks, cook in a nonstick pan with 1–2 tablespoons extra oil for 3–4 minutes, and then store.

MAKES ABOUT ¾ CUP (ENOUGH FOR 2–4 CURRIES)

Seafood

With such a diversity of raw ingredients available — fish from fresh and salt waters, shellfish, crustacea, cephalopods — the spectrum of seafood curry recipes is understandably vast and imaginative.

The seafood curries that follow feature tender fish fillets, banana-leaf parcels, meaty fish heads and spiny-shelled bug tails, rings and pouches of tender squid, plump prawns with tiger stripes. There is a taste for every palate, from mild, aromatic coconut-milk curry sauces to the spiciness of fresh basil and coriander, the tang of tamarind and lime juice, and as much (or as little) chilli heat as you like.

Unless otherwise specified, use a firm-fleshed fish such as snapper or blue-eye cod for curry dishes.

Prawn and tomato sambar

2–4 dried red chillies

2 cloves garlic, chopped

2-cm piece fresh ginger, chopped

1–2 fresh hot green chillies, deseeded and chopped

2 tablespoons fresh coriander leaves

2 tablespoons cumin seeds

½ teaspoon fennel seeds

3 tablespoons ghee

1 large onion, thinly sliced

½ teaspoon ground turmeric

2½ teaspoons sambar masala

350 g canned crushed tomatoes

750 g medium-sized green (raw) prawns in their shells

1 tablespoon soft brown sugar

1 tablespoon freshly squeezed lemon juice

chopped fresh dill, for garnish

Soak dried chillies in boiling water for 5-10 minutes, then slit open and remove seeds. Place in a mortar or small food processor with the garlic, ginger, green chillies and coriander leaves, and grind to a paste. Set aside.

In a small dry pan, roast the cumin and fennel seeds over medium heat until very aromatic and beginning to pop (about 3 minutes), then grind finely.

Heat the ghee in a medium-sized saucepan and fry the sliced onion until well coloured (about 4 minutes), stirring frequently. Add the prepared chilli paste and fry for a further 2 minutes, stirring continually, until very aromatic.

Next add the ground cumin, fennel and turmeric, and the sambar masala, and cook for 1 minute. Stir in the crushed tomatoes and simmer for 6 minutes.

Meanwhile, peel and devein the prawns.

Add prawns, sugar and lemon juice to the pan and cook just long enough for the prawns to turn pink and firm, and the flavours to meld together (about 3 minutes). Garnish with chopped dill just before serving.

SERVES 4−6

Tangy Goan coconut prawn curry

1 kg medium-sized green (raw) prawns in their shells

2 tablespoons vegetable oil

1 medium-sized onion, thinly sliced

2.5-cm piece fresh ginger, grated

2 fresh hot green chillies, deseeded and finely sliced

1 unripe mango, peeled and flesh finely sliced (optional)

1½ tablespoons ground coriander

½ teaspoon ground turmeric

¾ cup desiccated coconut

400 ml coconut cream

salt and white pepper

2 tablespoons finely chopped fresh coriander leaves

Shell and devein the prawns, leaving the tail fin attached.

Heat oil in a medium-sized saucepan and sauté the onion until soft and lightly coloured (about 5 minutes). Add ginger, chillies, mango, ground coriander and ground turmeric, and sauté briefly, stirring well.

Add desiccated coconut and 1 cup of the coconut cream to pan. Bring barely to the boil, then reduce heat and simmer for 10 minutes. Add prawns, remaining coconut cream, salt and pepper, and simmer over medium–low heat until the prawns are cooked (about 3 minutes). Stir in chopped coriander before serving.

SERVES 4–6

Green prawn curry

700 g large green (raw) prawns in their shells

2 tablespoons peanut or vegetable oil

½–1 tablespoon Thai Green Curry Paste (page 19)

440 ml coconut milk

3 kaffir lime leaves

90 g sliced bamboo shoots

1 small bunch Thai basil, leaves picked

1½ tablespoons fish sauce

1 teaspoon crushed palm sugar

salt and black pepper

fresh lime juice

Fill a saucepan with lightly salted water and bring to the boil. Add the prawns and cook for 5 minutes. Strain the liquid into another pan.

Peel prawns and set aside, covered. Add heads and shells to the strained liquid, simmer for 5 minutes and strain again. Reserve 1 cup of the liquid.

In a shallow pan heat the oil and fry the curry paste for 2–3 minutes, stirring continually. Add the coconut milk and ½–1 cup of the reserved prawn stock, to make a thin or slightly creamy sauce, as preferred. Simmer for 4–5 minutes until very fragrant.

Add the lime leaves and bamboo shoots to the pan with the reserved prawns. Simmer gently for 2–3 minutes, then stir in the basil leaves, fish sauce and sugar, and season to taste with salt, pepper and lime juice.

SERVES 4–6

Prawn and pumpkin curry

400 g pumpkin, peeled and cut into 1.5-cm cubes

1–2 dried chillies

1 teaspoon fenugreek seeds

1½ tablespoons coriander seeds

2 teaspoon cumin seeds

8 curry leaves

5 tablespoons desiccated coconut

1 teaspoon ground turmeric

1 medium-sized onion, quartered

2-cm piece fresh ginger, chopped

2 cloves garlic, chopped

2–3 tablespoons ghee, butter or oil

300 g peeled baby prawns

salt

1 tablespoon tamarind water or lemon juice

Boil the pumpkin for 6–8 minutes in lightly salted water, until almost cooked. Drain the pumpkin, reserving 1 cup of the water.

Mix the chillies, spices, curry leaves and coconut in a dry pan and toast, stirring frequently, until the coconut is evenly browned and the mixture very aromatic. Transfer immediately to a spice grinder and grind to a fine powder. Stir in the turmeric.

In a food processor grind the onion, ginger and garlic to a paste. >

Heat the ghee, butter or oil and sauté the onion paste for about 4 minutes, stirring frequently, until soft and fragrant. Add the ground spices and fry briefly, then pour in 1 cup of reserved pumpkin water and bring to a brisk boil. Reduce heat and simmer for 2–3 minutes to meld flavours.

Return the pumpkin to the pan, along with the prawns, salt and tamarind water or lemon juice to taste, and simmer for 1–2 minutes.

SERVES 4–6

A curry of prawns and green capsicum

600 g medium-sized green (raw) prawns, in their shells

2½ tablespoons ghee or oil

1 small cinnamon stick

2 bay leaves

1 large onion, very finely chopped

200 g canned crushed tomatoes

2 fresh green chillies, deseeded and very finely chopped

4 cloves garlic, very finely chopped

1-cm piece fresh ginger, very finely chopped

1½ teaspoons ground coriander

1 teaspoon ground cumin

1 teaspoon Garam Masala (page 18)

⅓ teaspoon ground turmeric

1 teaspoon salt

⅓ cup natural yoghurt

150 g green capsicum, trimmed and diced

4 tablespoons chopped fresh coriander leaves

Peel the prawns, leaving the tail fin intact. Place heads and shells in a small saucepan with cold water to cover, and bring to the boil. Reduce heat and simmer for 5 minutes, then strain and reserve ½ cup of the liquid. Devein the prawns and set aside. >

Put the ghee or oil into a shallow pan and add the cinnamon stick and bay leaves. When the oil is hot, add the onion and fry until lightly browned, then reduce heat and add the tomatoes, chillies, garlic, ginger, spices and salt. Bring to boil and simmer for 5–6 minutes, then remove from heat and set aside to cool for 10 minutes.

In a small bowl mix the yoghurt with ½ cup of the reserved prawn water. Stir into the curry and simmer for 5 minutes. Add the prawns and green capsicum and simmer for a further 5-6 minutes. Check seasonings, and stir in chopped coriander before serving.

SERVES 4–6

Prawns in fiery red sauce

1 medium onion, chopped

4 cloves garlic, chopped

1-cm piece fresh ginger, chopped

¼ cup vegetable oil

1 cinnamon stick

6 cardamom pods, cracked

2 bay leaves

2 teaspoons ground coriander

1½ teaspoons ground cumin

1½ cups canned crushed tomatoes

½ teaspoon ground turmeric

1–2 teaspoons sambal ulek

1 teaspoon tomato paste

⅓ cup natural yoghurt

350 g small peeled prawns

Garam Masala (page 18)

Process the onion, garlic and ginger to a smooth paste. Heat the oil in a pan and fry cinnamon, cardamom and bay leaves for 30 seconds over medium-high heat, then add the onion paste and cook for 5 minutes, stirring. Add the ground coriander and cumin and stir for about 30 seconds, then pour in the tomatoes, turmeric, sambal ulek and tomato paste, and bring to the boil. Simmer for about 3 minutes until the flavours mellow, then add the yoghurt a tablespoon at a time, cooking for 30 seconds between each addition, until it is all incorporated.

Add a little water if the sauce seems too thick. Add the prawns and cook gently for 3 minutes. Serve in bowls, with a sprinkle of garam masala.

SERVES 4

Spicy prawn noodle curry

1 small cucumber, finely sliced

¾ cup bean sprouts, blanched
and drained

2 cups shredded Chinese
cabbage, blanched and
drained

4 cups coconut milk

1 cup fish stock

2 fresh hot red chillies,
slit open and deseeded

2-cm piece fresh ginger,
chopped

4 spring onions, chopped
(reserve some green tops
for garnish)

2 cloves garlic, sliced

salt and lemon or lime juice,
to taste

500 g fresh rice noodles

500 g medium-sized green (raw)
prawns, shelled and deveined

Arrange the cucumber, bean sprouts and cabbage in individual dishes and
set on a tray to serve as accompaniments.

Bring the coconut milk to a rapid boil in a medium-sized pan and add fish
stock, chillies, ginger, spring onions and garlic. Bring back to the boil, then
simmer for about 10 minutes, until the flavours have blended. Season to
taste with salt and a big squeeze of lemon or lime juice.

Meanwhile, rinse the noodles in warm water and divide between heated
serving bowls. >

Add the prawns to the pan and simmer for about 3 minutes, then divide between the bowls, and strain the hot curry gravy over.

Serve the tray of prepared accompaniments with the curry.

Sliced hardboiled egg, blanched baby bok choy, crisp-fried onions and pickled shallots would also go well with this curry.

SERVES 4−6

Balti prawns

2 tablespoons ghee or oil

2 cloves garlic, crushed

1 large onion, thinly sliced

2 tablespoons mild Indian
curry paste

3 teaspoons tomato paste

700 g green (raw) prawns,
shelled and deveined

1 green capsicum,
trimmed and diced

1 fresh hot red chilli,
deseeded and sliced

1 fresh hot green chilli,
deseeded and sliced

salt

sugar

In a non-stick pan heat the ghee or oil and fry the garlic and onion until well softened (about 5 minutes). Add the curry and tomato pastes, and stir over medium heat for 1½ minutes. Add the prawns, capsicum and chillies, and cook, stirring almost constantly, until the prawns are pink and the capsicum softened (about 3 minutes). (Add a tablespoon of water from time to time, if needed, to prevent the onions sticking.)

Season to taste with salt and sugar. Serve with rice and flat bread.

SERVES 4–6

Seafood laksa

5 dried red chillies

1 tablespoon coriander seeds

1 teaspoon cumin seeds

1 tablespoon macadamia
or cashew nuts

1 teaspoon ground turmeric

2 teaspoons shrimp paste

1-cm piece fresh ginger, chopped

1 tablespoon fresh coriander
(roots and stems)

1 stalk lemongrass, chopped

3 tablespoons vegetable oil

2 cups coconut milk

100 g shelled and deveined
prawns

100 g squid, cut into rings

100 g frozen fishballs, cut in half

8 mussels in their shells
(optional)

1 cup coconut cream

salt or fish sauce

black pepper

sugar

120 g rice vermicelli

60 g fresh hokkien noodles

180 g bean sprouts

1 small cucumber, deseeded
and thinly sliced

1–3 fresh red chillies, deseeded
and chopped

3 kaffir lime leaves, finely
shredded

fresh Vietnamese mint or
basil leaves

To make the curry sauce, toast the chillies, coriander, cumin and nuts in a
dry pan over medium heat until aromatic and beginning to pop. Transfer to
a spice grinder and grind to a fine powder. Add the turmeric. >

Wrap the shrimp paste in a piece of foil and roast in the same pan for 1 minute, turning several times. In a mortar now grind the ginger, coriander and lemongrass to a coarse paste. Add the roasted shrimp paste and grind again briefly.

Heat the oil in a wok or pan and fry the paste mixture for 1 minute, stirring constantly. Add the ground spices and fry for 30 seconds, then add the coconut milk and bring to the boil. Simmer for about 12 minutes until flavours are well blended.

Add the prawns, squid, fishballs and mussels (if using) to the pan, with half the coconut cream, plus salt and fish sauce to taste, and a little pepper and sugar. Simmer gently until seafood is cooked (about 3 minutes).

Now cook the vermicelli and hokkien noodles for 1 minute in boiling water. Add the bean sprouts, stir for 30 seconds, and drain.

Divide the noodles and bean sprouts between four bowls, and add cucumber and chillies. Distribute the seafood and hot sauce evenly between the bowls and drizzle a little of the remaining coconut cream over. Serve garnished with shredded lime leaves and a few herb leaves.

SERVES 4

Prawn cakes in spicy tomato sauce

500 g green (raw) prawn meat

½ teaspoon ground hot chilli

2 tablespoons chopped onion

2 cloves garlic, chopped

1 teaspoon salt

2 cups vegetable oil

½ teaspoon fenugreek seeds

¾ teaspoon brown mustard seeds

8 curry leaves (optional)

1 fresh hot red chilli, deseeded and very finely chopped

2 extra cloves garlic, very finely chopped

2 teaspoons very finely chopped fresh ginger

1 extra onion, very thinly sliced

250 g canned crushed tomatoes

Place the prawn meat in a food processor with the ground chilli, onion, garlic and salt, and grind to a paste. With wet hands form into walnut-sized balls, and flatten each slightly.

In a pan heat the oil to medium-hot and fry the prawn cakes for about 2 minutes, until just cooked through. Lift out and drain on paper towels. Pour off all but 3 tablespoons of the oil and fry the fenugreek and mustard seeds with the curry leaves (if using) until they pop. Add the fresh chilli, garlic, ginger and sliced onion and fry until very aromatic and lightly browned. Add the tomatoes and simmer for 5–6 minutes, adding a little cold water if sauce is too thick. Check seasonings. Gently heat the prawn cakes in the sauce, and serve.

SERVES 6

Fish tikka masala

500 g swordfish or other firm
   white fish, cut into 2-cm cubes

juice of ½ lemon

1 teaspoon salt

½ cup natural yoghurt

2 cloves garlic, crushed

½ teaspoon crushed fresh ginger

3 teaspoons tandoori paste

8 curry leaves

ghee or oil

1 tablespoon chopped fresh
   coriander leaves

Garam Masala (page 18)

lime wedges

Place fish in a dish and season with lemon juice and salt. Cover with plastic wrap and set aside for 5–10 minutes. If using bamboo skewers (rather than metal ones), soak them in water for 10–20 minutes.

In a bowl combine the yoghurt with garlic, ginger and tandoori paste and spread evenly over the fish. Marinate for at least 30 minutes, turning occasionally. Thread the fish onto skewers, including a curry leaf on each, and grill for 6–8 minutes on a barbecue hotplate, under a preheated grill, or over gently glowing coals, turning and brushing occasionally with melted ghee or oil.

Serve skewers on a platter, sprinkled with coriander and garam masala, and with lime wedges on the side.

SERVES 4

Indonesian banana-leaf baked fish

1 kg whole fish, e.g. snapper,
    coral trout

1 tablespoon tamarind water
    or lemon juice

1 teaspoon salt

2-cm piece fresh ginger, grated

1 teaspoon shrimp paste

1½ teaspoons sambal ulek

1 teaspoon soft brown sugar
    or palm sugar

1 garlic clove, crushed

¾ cup desiccated coconut

½ cup coconut cream

Preheat oven to 200°C, if using (you can also cook this dish in a covered barbecue).

Clean and scale the fish and make deep slashes across each side at 2-cm intervals. In a bowl combine the remaining ingredients to make a thick paste. Spread half the paste evenly over one side of the fish.

Tear off a piece of aluminium foil at least 15 cm longer than the fish, and spread pieces of banana leaf along the centre. Brush the leaves with oil, then place the fish on the leaves, seasoned side down. Spread the remaining paste over the top of the fish and fold the leaves over. Gather the edges of the foil together and fold securely to encase the fish.

Cook fish parcel in preheated oven or in a covered barbecue for about 20 minutes, then remove and carefully open the foil. Separate the banana leaves and test if the fish is cooked by inserting the point of a knife in the thickest part near the head. It is cooked when the flesh is opaque and flakes easily. (If not quite done, reseal and let rest for 10 minutes to cook in the residual heat of the foil, or return to the oven for 5–6 minutes.)

When cooked, discard foil and lift fish onto a serving dish.

SERVES 4–6

Green masala fish

1 × 600-g whole fish
   (e.g. snapper)

salt

1 cup peanut or vegetable oil

1 onion, very thinly sliced

4–5 garlic cloves, crushed

2-cm piece fresh ginger, grated

3 fresh green chillies, deseeded
   and very finely chopped

1½ cups chopped fresh
   coriander leaves (include
   some stems)

1 teaspoon ground cumin

1 teaspoon fennel seeds

extra fresh coriander leaves,
   for garnish

Clean and scale the fish and rinse thoroughly, drain well and dry with paper towel. Make several deep slashes across each side and rub with salt.

Heat 3 tablespoons of the oil in a large, shallow pan and fry the onions until very soft (about 5 minutes), then retrieve with a slotted spoon and transfer to a food processor.

Add remaining oil to the pan and fry the fish over high heat for 3 minutes on each side, until the skin is slightly crisp. Lift out carefully, drain and set aside. >

Add the garlic, ginger, chillies and coriander leaves to the food processor with the cooked onion and grind to a smooth paste. Drain the oil from the pan, spoon in the onion paste and fry over medium heat for 3-4 minutes, stirring frequently. Add the spices and 1 cup of water and bring to the boil, then reduce heat and simmer for 2–3 minutes.

Return the fish to the pan and gently simmer in the sauce until cooked through, carefully turning once, or frequently basting with the sauce. To serve, carefully slide fish onto a platter. Garnish with extra coriander just before serving.

SERVES 4

Malaysian seafood and cabbage quick curry

6 shallots, finely chopped

1 clove garlic, finely chopped

2 tablespoons vegetable oil

½ teaspoon ground turmeric

2–3 teaspoons mild Malaysian
curry paste

440 ml coconut milk

2 cups Chinese cabbage,
finely shredded

150 g small peeled prawns

150 g cleaned squid,
cut into rings

about 130 g firm white fish, cubed

salt

Sauté the shallots and garlic in the oil for 1 minute, stirring. Add the turmeric and curry paste and stir for another minute, then add the coconut milk and the cabbage and simmer for about 5 minutes, covered.

Add the seafood, and salt to taste, and again simmer covered for about 4 minutes, until the seafood and cabbage are tender.

SERVES 4

Green curry of seafood

½–1½ tablespoons Thai Green
  Curry Paste (page 20)

1 tablespoon oil

1½ cups coconut milk

½ cup fish stock or water

½ teaspoon fennel seeds

1 stalk lemongrass, slit
  lengthways

8 small green beans, snow peas
  or sugarsnap peas

1 medium-sized carrot, sliced

1 small zucchini, thickly sliced

4 large green (raw) prawns,
  in their shells

4 mussels in their shells

1 × 200-g salmon steak, skinned
  and cut into 4 pieces

4 kaffir lime leaves

4 baby squid, cleaned

⅓ cup sliced bamboo shoots

sugar

fish sauce

4 cherry or grape tomatoes,
  halved

fresh basil leaves

Sauté the curry paste in the oil for 2 minutes. Add the coconut milk and
fish stock or water, fennel seeds and lemongrass, and simmer for 5–6
minutes.

In a small saucepan boil the beans, carrot and zucchini in lightly salted
water until nearly tender. Drain vegetables and set aside.

Add the prawns and mussels to the curry sauce and poach for 2 minutes. Add the salmon, lime leaves, squid and bamboo shoots, and poach at a gentle simmer for 2 minutes. Add the boiled vegetables, sugar and fish sauce to taste, the cherry tomatoes and basil leaves and warm through in the sauce.

To serve, divide the ingredients evenly between four heated bowls and pour sauce over.

SERVES 4

Tomato and onion fish from Bengal

1 small whole fish, or 600 g thick
   fish fillets cut into fingers

plain flour

1 cup ghee or mustard oil

400 g canned crushed tomatoes

4 garlic cloves, crushed

1 large onion, thinly sliced

1 teaspoon ground chilli

2 teaspoons sugar

1 tablespoon fresh lime juice

2 fresh green chillies, deseeded
   and sliced

3 roma tomatoes, cut lengthways
   into wedges

2–3 slices fresh ginger, finely
   shredded

sprigs of fresh coriander or dill

Clean and scale the whole fish (if using). Dust the fish or fillets with flour. Heat ghee or mustard oil in a wide pan and fry the fish until crisped on the surface, but not completely cooked through (about 4 minutes). Remove and set aside.

Pour off all but 2 tablespoons of the ghee or oil and add to the pan the tomatoes, garlic, onion and chilli powder or paprika. Simmer until thick and soft, then transfer to a saucepan large enough to hold the fish. Add sugar, juice, chillies, tomatoes and ginger, and the fish. Simmer gently, basting fish with the sauce, for about 4 minutes until tender and heated through.

Transfer to a serving dish and garnish with herbs.

SERVES 4–6

Tandoori-roasted John Dory

500 g John Dory or other flat
   fish, such as flounder

1½ teaspoons cumin seeds

¼ teaspoon fennel seeds

¼ teaspoon ajwain or
   caraway seeds

1 fresh green chilli, deseeded
   and chopped

1 clove garlic, chopped

1-cm piece fresh ginger,
   chopped

½ medium-sized onion, chopped

1 teaspoon salt

1 tablespoon fresh lemon juice

⅓ cup natural yoghurt

vegetable oil

Preheat the oven or grill to its highest temperature. Line a baking tray
with baking paper or foil and place a wire cake rack over the tray.

Clean, scale and rinse the fish, and drain well. Clip the fins and make
several deep slashes diagonally across each side.

Warm the spices in a dry pan until fragrant (about 1½ minutes), and then
grind finely. In a mortar or small food processor, grind the chilli, garlic,
ginger, onion and salt to a paste. Add the ground spices, lemon juice,
yoghurt and 2 teaspoons of oil.

Spoon some of the marinade into the cavity of the fish, then spread the
remainder evenly on the outside. Cover with plastic wrap and refrigerate
for several hours. >

Place the fish on the prepared tray and cook for about 6 minutes on each side, basting with a little more oil during cooking. Transfer carefully to a serving plate and accompany with freshly sliced onion and lemon wedges.

Its firm skin and thin fillets make John Dory a fish well suited to the intense heat of a tandoori oven. A closed barbecue or domestic oven on the highest setting will give more than acceptable results.

SERVES 4

Coconut fish curry with crisp shallots

6 thick pieces white fish

2 cups coconut milk

1 teaspoon salt

⅓ cup thinly sliced shallots

½ cup vegetable oil

1 tablespoon finely chopped
fresh red chilli

2 teaspoons finely chopped
fresh ginger

1 teaspoon ground turmeric

1½ teaspoons shrimp paste,
mashed

1 tablespoon tamarind water

2 teaspoons sugar

black pepper

Place fish in a wide shallow pan with the coconut milk and salt, and simmer gently for about 10 minutes, until the fish is tender. Carefully transfer the fish to a serving dish, cover with foil and set aside. Reserve coconut milk.

In another pan fry the shallots in the oil until crisp and well browned. Lift out with a slotted spoon and drain on paper towels. Pour off all but 2 tablespoons of the oil and fry the chilli and ginger for 1 minute, stirring constantly. Add the turmeric and shrimp paste and stir for another minute.

Pour in the reserved coconut milk, add the tamarind water, sugar and pepper, and bring almost to the boil. Simmer for about 8 minutes, until well reduced and aromatic. Pour over the fish and scatter with the fried shallots before serving.

SERVES 6

Thai fish dumpling curry

500 g fine-textured white fish, cubed

½ teaspoon salt

3–5 dried red chillies, soaked for 15 minutes in hot water

2 cloves garlic, chopped

6–8 shallots, chopped

2 sprigs fresh coriander, including roots and stems

1-cm piece fresh ginger, chopped

1 stalk lemongrass, chopped

1 teaspoon shrimp paste

2 tablespoons vegetable oil

2–3 tablespoons fish sauce

fresh lime juice

torn fresh basil leaves

In a food processor grind the cubed fish with salt and 3–4 tablespoons of cold water. When mixture is soft and pasty, use wet hands to form into walnut-sized balls.

Bring a saucepan of lightly salted water to the boil and poach the fish dumplings until they float to the surface (about 2 minutes). Remove with a slotted spoon and drain, reserving the water.

Drain soaked chillies, and deseed. In a small food processor or a mortar, grind the chillies with the garlic, shallots, coriander, ginger, lemongrass and shrimp paste, adding the vegetable oil to help blend the ingredients to a smooth paste. Tip mixture into a dry pan and sauté gently for 2–3 minutes, until very fragrant, stirring continually.

Add the fish dumplings to the pan with enough water to just cover, and simmer for 2–3 minutes. Season to taste with fish sauce and lime juice, and add the basil leaves just before serving.

SERVES 4–6

Crisp-fried fish in hot curry sauce

1¼ tablespoons Thai Red Curry Paste (page 19)

1½ cups coconut cream

1½ tablespoons fish sauce

2 teaspoons palm sugar or soft brown sugar

30 g dried shrimp or fish, ground to fluff in a food processor (optional)

oil for deep-frying

400 g thin fish fillets

plain flour, rice flour or corn flour

fresh coriander sprigs

In a small pan simmer the curry paste in the coconut cream for about 8 minutes, until aromatic and the flavours have mellowed. Add the fish sauce and sugar, and simmer for another few minutes. Stir in the ground shrimp or fish, if using.

Heat oil for deep-frying to medium-hot. Cut the fish into pieces about 5 cm × 4 cm and coat very lightly with flour. Deep-fry fish until crisp and well browned on the surface. Lift out with a slotted spoon, drain briefly on a paper towel, and place on a serving dish.

Spoon the hot sauce over and serve garnished with coriander.

SERVES 6

Spicy baked fish

1.3 kg snapper

salt and black pepper

1 tablespoon fresh lemon juice or tamarind water

⅓ cup cashew nuts

1 teaspoon ground turmeric

½ teaspoon shrimp paste

1.5-cm piece fresh ginger, chopped

1 medium onion, chopped

1–2 fresh hot red chillies, deseeded and roughly chopped

3 cloves garlic, chopped

2 tomatoes, deseeded, chopped and well drained

1 teaspoon sugar

3–4 tablespoons chopped fresh coriander

vegetable oil

Preheat oven to 180°C.

Clean, scale and rinse the fish. Dry with paper towel and make several deep diagonal slashes on each side. Season with salt, pepper and lemon juice or tamarind water, and set aside.

Process or grind the cashews, turmeric and shrimp paste to a paste. Grind the ginger, onion, chillies and garlic to a paste and combine with the cashew paste. Grind together briefly. Add the tomatoes, sugar and coriander and process to a thick paste. Add 2 tablespoons vegetable oil and mix again.

Brush a piece of aluminium foil with oil. Spread half the paste over one side of the fish, with a little in the cavity. Place fish on the foil, coated side down, then spread the remaining paste over the other side. Fold the foil around the fish and seal, then place in preheated oven on a wire rack placed over a baking tray.

Bake in oven for about 25 minutes, or cook on a barbecue over medium heat, turning several times. To test if fish is done, open the foil and insert the point of a knife into the thickest part of the fish, behind the head. If cooked, flesh will be opaque and flake easily. Open the foil, increase the heat and cook for a few more minutes to crisp the top.

SERVES 8–10

Javanese spiced fish

500 g fillets of mackerel or other oily fish

1 large onion, grated

3 cloves garlic, crushed with 1 teaspoon salt

2-cm piece fresh ginger, grated

1 teaspoon shrimp paste

2 tablespoons peanut oil

2 teaspoons sambal ulek

1 tablespoon tamarind water or fresh lemon juice

1 cup coconut cream

salt

sugar (optional)

chopped fresh herbs (basil, dill, coriander)

crisp-fried garlic (optional)

Holding the knife at an angle, cut the fish into escalopes 1 cm thick, and place in a dish. Hold a fine nylon sieve over a bowl and put in it the grated onion and its juice, the crushed garlic and the grated ginger and its juice. Press with the back of a wooden spoon to extract as much juice as possible, and save both the liquid and the remaining solids.

Mash the shrimp paste and fry in 1 tablespoon of the peanut oil. Add to the pressed juices, along with the sambal ulek, tamarind water or lemon juice, and coconut cream, and mix to a thick paste. Spread over the fish, turning so each piece is evenly coated. Leave for 20–30 minutes. >

Heat the remaining oil in a wide non-stick pan over medium heat. Scrape surplus marinade from the fish and reserve. Cook the fish, turning once, until just tender (about 1½ minutes each side). Transfer to a serving dish.

Add the reserved onion, garlic and ginger solids to the pan and stir-fry for 2 minutes, until fragrant. Pour in the remaining marinade, add a little water and simmer briskly for about 4 minutes. Season to taste with salt and, if you like, a little sugar.

Spoon sauce over the fish, scatter with chopped herbs and crisp-fried garlic, if using, and serve.

SERVES 4−6

Fish-head curry

2–4 large fish heads

3 cloves garlic, chopped

1 small onion, halved

2–4 fresh red chillies, deseeded
and chopped

small bunch of coriander

1 teaspoon shrimp paste

2 tablespoons vegetable oil

600 ml coconut cream

2 extra onions, sliced

2-cm piece fresh galangal
or ginger, chopped

8 curry leaves (optional)

2 large very ripe tomatoes,
deseeded and chopped

4 spring onions, sliced

1 tablespoon tamarind water

½ teaspoon fennel seeds

salt and black pepper

Rinse the fish heads and strain in a colander.

In a spice grinder or small processor place the garlic, onion, chillies, coriander roots and stems (save the leaves for garnish), shrimp paste and oil. Grind to a paste.

Measure 3 tablespoons of coconut cream into a large pot or wok and add the seasoning paste. Cook, stirring constantly, for about 4 minutes. Add the sliced onions, spreading them evenly over the bottom of the pan. Put in the drained fish heads, add the galangal, curry leaves (if using), tomatoes, spring onions, remaining coconut milk and enough water to barely cover. >

Cover the pan and bring almost to the boil, reduce heat and simmer for 10 minutes. Add the tamarind water, fennel seeds, salt and pepper to taste, and half the coriander leaves. Simmer for another 10 minutes, or until the flesh is falling from the fish bones. Lift bones onto plate and pick off any remaining meat, then return this to the pot.

The soft flesh in the area behind the head of a large fish is often overlooked in the cleaning process. But canny Singaporean cooks have made an art of this prized leftover.

SERVES 6

Little spicy fish parcels

10–12 squares banana leaf, each 12 cm × 10 cm (or use aluminium foil)

vegetable oil

400 g white fish fillets

1 cup freshly grated coconut

1 onion, chopped

2 cloves garlic, chopped

1-cm piece fresh ginger, chopped

2–4 sprigs fresh coriander

2–3 teaspoons sambal ulek

1 teaspoon salt

½–1 teaspoon ground turmeric

Lightly brush the banana leaves (or foil) with oil. Cut the fish into 10–12 pieces of even size.

In a food processor blend the coconut, onion, garlic, ginger, coriander, sambal ulek, salt and turmeric until it forms a smooth paste. Spread mixture over one side of each piece of fish and place in the centre of banana leaf or foil, seasoned side down. Cover upper side of fish with the remaining paste.

Fold the leaf or foil into a parcel (secure leaf with toothpicks). Cook on a hot grill for about 5 minutes, turning frequently.

Serve the parcels on a platter or on individual plates, to be unwrapped at the table.

MAKES 10–12

Yellow curry of fish

300 g firm fish fillets

1½ tablespoons vegetable or peanut oil

1 tablespoon yellow curry paste

3 kaffir lime leaves

1 fresh hot red chilli, deseeded and sliced

1 tablespoon fish sauce

1½ cups coconut milk

¼ cup sliced bamboo shoots

2 tablespoons Thai pea eggplants (optional)

2 spring onions, sliced

4 green beans, sliced and parboiled

fresh Thai basil leaves

salt and black pepper

Cut the fish into thick slices and set aside.

Heat the oil in a pan and sauté the curry paste until very fragrant (about 2 minutes). Add the lime leaves, chilli, fish sauce and coconut milk, and bring quickly to the boil. Simmer for 2 minutes.

Add the fish to the pan, reduce heat and simmer gently for 2–3 minutes. Add bamboo shoots, pea eggplants (if using), spring onions and green beans, and simmer for 3–4 minutes.

Just before serving, stir in basil leaves and season to taste with salt and pepper.

SERVES 4–6

Ginger yoghurt fish curry

1 teaspoon ground turmeric

1 teaspoon salt

2 teaspoons ground coriander

½ teaspoon ground cumin

½ teaspoon ground chilli

1 tablespoon fresh lemon juice

1 cup natural yoghurt

700 g thick, soft-fleshed
   white fish

1 onion, chopped

1 fresh hot red chilli, deseeded
   and sliced

1 teaspoon crushed garlic

2 tablespoons vegetable oil

2 tablespoons thick cream

1–2 tablespoons sweet ginger
   in syrup, chopped

In a dish large enough to hold the fish in one layer, mix the turmeric, salt, coriander, cumin, chilli powder, lemon juice and yoghurt. Add the fish and stir to coat evenly.

In a non-stick pan fry the onion, sliced chilli and garlic in the oil until softened and lightly coloured (about 4 minutes). Brush the marinade from the fish, add to the pan with 1 cup water and simmer for about 6 minutes, until the sauce is fragrant and the onion very soft.

Slide the fish into the sauce and simmer for 5 minutes. Add the cream and ginger (with its syrup) and continue cooking until the fish is tender.

SERVES 4–6

Coconut fish molee

700 g fish (e.g. snapper, bass)

2 tablespoons vegetable oil

1 large onion, sliced

3–6 fresh green chillies,
  deseeded and sliced

4 cloves garlic, crushed

1-cm piece fresh ginger,
  shredded

400 ml coconut milk

1 large tomato, deseeded and
  sliced

12 curry leaves

1 teaspoon ground turmeric

2 tablespoons freshly grated
  or desiccated coconut

2 large leaves Chinese cabbage,
  or a few handfuls spinach
  leaves

fresh lime or lemon juice

salt and freshly ground white
  pepper

Cut the fish into 4-cm cubes.

Heat the oil in a shallow pan and fry the onion, chillies, garlic and ginger until onion is well softened but only lightly coloured (about 5 minutes). Add 1 cup water, the coconut milk, tomato, curry leaves, turmeric, coconut and fish pieces, and simmer gently until fish is almost tender.

Finely shred the cabbage leaves (slice spinach if the leaves are large). Add to the curry and simmer for 3–4 minutes, until tender. Add lime or lemon juice to taste and season with salt and white pepper.

SERVES 6

Jungle curry of fish and vegetables

6 birdseye chillies

½ stalk lemongrass

1-cm piece fresh galangal
   or ginger, chopped

5 red or brown shallots, chopped

5 cloves garlic, chopped

1 teaspoon shrimp paste

2-3 coriander roots

4 tablespoons vegetable oil

2 slender Asian eggplants,
   quartered lengthways

2 cups fish stock

1 bamboo shoot, chopped

1 snake bean or 4 green beans,
   sliced

1 zucchini, thickly sliced (or use
   ½ choko, cut into chunks)

300 g firm white fish fillets,
   cut into 2-cm cubes

3–4 kaffir lime leaves

salt and/or fish sauce, to taste

a handful fresh basil leaves

Process or grind first 7 ingredients to a smooth paste.

Heat half the vegetable oil in a pan and fry the eggplants until lightly coloured on the cut surfaces, then remove to paper towels to drain.

Heat remaining oil and sauté the spice paste for about 2 minutes, stirring constantly to prevent catching. Pour in the stock, bring to the boil and simmer for about 7 minutes, until flavours have mellowed. >

Add the bamboo shoot, beans and zucchini or choko, and simmer for about 4 minutes, until almost cooked. Add fish pieces and lime leaves and simmer gently for 5–6 minutes, adding a little more stock or water if needed. Season to taste with salt and/or fish sauce and stir in basil leaves just before serving.

SERVES 4

Goa fish curry

750 g mackerel or swordfish
   steaks

juice of ½ lemon or lime

1 teaspoon ground turmeric

1 teaspoon salt

4–6 fresh hot red chillies,
   deseeded

1 onion, cut in half

2-cm piece fresh ginger,
   chopped

4 cloves garlic, chopped

2 tablespoons vegetable oil

1 tablespoon tamarind water

1 large very ripe tomato,
   deseeded and sliced

2 teaspoons tomato paste

1½ teaspoons ground sweet
   paprika

1 tablespoon ground coriander

1 teaspoon ground cumin

½ teaspoon crushed fennel
   seeds

1 cup coconut cream

chopped fresh herbs
   (e.g. coriander, dill, mint)

Cut the fish into 2-cm cubes and place in a dish with the lemon or lime juice, turmeric and salt. Mix well and leave to marinate for 15 minutes.

Process or grind half the onion with the ginger and garlic, until it forms a smooth paste. Finely slice the remaining onion half. >

Heat the oil in a shallow pan and fry the sliced onion until well coloured (about 7 minutes). Add the ground paste and fry until fragrant (about 3 minutes), then add the tamarind water, tomato, tomato paste and spices and stir over medium heat for 2–3 minutes.

Add the fish and coconut cream to the pan, with enough water to barely cover the fish, and bring to the boil. Reduce heat and simmer gently until the fish is very tender (about 12 minutes).

Stir in the chopped herbs just before serving.

SERVES 6

Crab curry

2 × 750-g crabs

2½ teaspoons crushed garlic

1 tablespoon sliced galangal

1–3 fresh red chillies, deseeded and chopped

1 teaspoon shrimp paste

4 candlenuts or 8 macadamias

1 teaspoon salt

1 teaspoon ground turmeric

4 tablespoons vegetable oil

6 red or brown shallots, finely sliced

2 stalks lemongrass, slit lengthways

2 cups thin coconut milk

1 tablespoon tamarind water or fresh lime juice

fresh coriander leaves

Clean the crabs, discarding inedible parts. Snap off the claws. With a cleaver or heavy knife cut claws in half, then cut crab into portions, each with one leg. Use the butt of the knife to crack the shells.

In a small food processor, or a mortar, grind the garlic, galangal, chillies, shrimp paste, nuts, salt and turmeric to a paste. Heat the oil in a wide pan and fry the paste for 2 minutes, stirring. >

Add the shallots, lemongrass, crab pieces and coconut milk to the pan and bring to boil, then reduce heat and simmer gently for about 15 minutes, until the crab is cooked and the sauce reduced.

Season to taste with tamarind water or lime juice, and garnish with the coriander leaves.

SERVES 6

Cochin fish curry

4 cloves garlic, chopped

1 cup freshly grated coconut (or use ¾ cup desiccated coconut soaked in ½ cup coconut milk)

½ teaspoon ground turmeric

3 tablespoons vegetable oil

½ teaspoon brown mustard seeds

8 shallots, finely sliced

2–4 fresh hot green chillies, deseeded and very finely sliced

3–4 pieces dried kokum rind (or 1 tablespoon tamarind water)

3–5 curry leaves

360 g white fish fillets, cubed

salt

sugar

Grind or process the garlic to a paste with the coconut and turmeric.

Heat the oil in a medium-sized pan and fry the mustard seeds for about 40 seconds on high heat, until they pop. Add the shallots and chillies and fry for 2 minutes, stirring. Add the kokum or tamarind, the curry leaves and 2 cups of water and bring to the boil. Simmer for 2 minutes, then add garlic-coconut paste and simmer for 5 minutes.

Add the fish and cook gently until tender, about 4 minutes. Season to taste with salt and a little sugar if needed, and serve.

SERVES 4–6

Tandoori bug tails

8 fresh Moreton Bay bugs (or 16
   large raw prawns, shelled)

1 small onion

4-cm piece fresh ginger

2 cloves garlic, crushed with
   1 teaspoon salt

1 teaspoon ground sweet paprika

½ cup natural yoghurt

2 teaspoons Garam Masala
   (page 18)

1 teaspoon yellow food colouring

juice of ½ lemon

melted ghee or vegetable oil

½ teaspoon ajwain or celery seeds

chopped fresh coriander

lime wedges

Preheat oven, grill or barbecue to very hot. Remove the bug tails from their shells and cut each in half lengthways (leave prawns whole if using). Place in a dish.

Grate the onion and ginger onto a piece of clean fine cloth and squeeze the juices into a bowl. Add the garlic paste, paprika, yoghurt, garam masala and food colouring. Add lemon juice and mix thoroughly. Spoon mixture over the bug tails or prawns and mix well to evenly coat. Set aside for 20–30 minutes.

Thread four half bug tails (or 4 prawns) onto each skewer. Brush with melted ghee or oil, and cook for about 4 minutes, turning frequently. Arrange the skewers on serving plates, and sprinkle with ajwain or celery seeds and the chopped coriander. Serve with lime wedges.

SERVES 4

Malaysian curried squid

500 g cleaned squid tubes

1 tablespoon tamarind water

1 small onion, very finely
chopped

2 cloves garlic, very finely
chopped

1-cm piece fresh ginger,
very finely chopped

1 tablespoon hot Malaysian
curry paste

1 teaspoon shrimp paste

1½ tablespoons peanut oil

salt and black pepper

sugar

1 cup coconut cream

Cut squid open and use the point of a sharp knife to score inside surface
in a cross-hatch pattern. Cut the squid into 4-cm squares, then place in
a dish with the tamarind water and 1 tablespoon water, and leave for
10 minutes.

In a medium saucepan sauté the onion, garlic, ginger, curry paste and
shrimp paste in the peanut oil. When very fragrant (about 3 minutes), add
the squid. Stir-fry for 30 seconds, then season with salt, pepper, a pinch
of sugar, and add the coconut cream.

Simmer gently over very low heat for about 20 minutes, stirring occasionally
and adding a little water from time to time if the sauce becomes too thick
and begins to stick.

SERVES 4–6

Chicken and duck

Tender and subtle in flavour, chicken is a perfect vehicle for curry spices and sauces. Indian and Sri Lankan cuisines offer kaleidoscopic variety in chicken curries: in India, from delicately spiced creamy kormas in the north to the vibrant curries of Chettinad in the south; in Sri Lanka, from richly roasted spices of the south island to the tart, hot flavours of the central coastal regions.

Malaysian, Burmese, Indonesian and Thai cooks equally appreciate the versatility of chicken, slicing and dicing it into their tangy green, red and yellow curries.

Richer than chicken, duck is also a favourite ingredient in curries, marrying well with bold, intense flavours and hot, hot chillies.

Coconut chicken curry

4 dried red chillies

3 tablespoons ghee

1.2 kg chicken pieces

1 large onion, finely chopped

3 cloves garlic, finely chopped

1½ teaspoons crushed fresh
  ginger

6–10 curry leaves

1½ tablespoons ground coriander

2 teaspoons ground cumin

1 teaspoon ground chilli
  (optional)

1½ cups chopped tomatoes

½ cup tamarind water

1 stalk lemongrass, split
  lengthways

1½ cups coconut milk

salt and black pepper

Soak chillies in hot water for 10 minutes, then drain, deseed and chop.

Heat ghee in a large frying pan and brown chicken pieces, then transfer to
a heavy saucepan. In the same frying pan sauté the onion, garlic, chillies,
ginger and curry leaves for 3–5 minutes, stirring. Add the coriander, cumin
and chilli powder (if using), and fry briefly, then add the tomatoes, tamarind
water, lemongrass and coconut milk and bring barely to the boil. Pour over
the chicken and add salt and pepper.

Cover saucepan and cook gently for about 30 minutes, until chicken
is falling from the bones. Remove lemongrass before serving.

SERVES 6

Chicken in yoghurt curry sauce

1.5 kg chicken pieces,
  on the bone

1 fresh green chilli, deseeded
  and roughly chopped

1.5-cm piece fresh ginger,
  chopped

2 garlic cloves, chopped

1 cup natural yoghurt

1 teaspoon salt

⅓ cup ghee or vegetable oil

¾ cup water

2–3 tablespoons chopped
  fresh coriander

Prick the chicken skin with a sharp skewer (this allows seasonings to penetrate) and place in a dish.

Grind the chilli, ginger and garlic to a smooth paste and mix with the yoghurt and salt. Spread evenly over the chicken and leave to marinate for several hours.

When ready to cook the chicken, use a pastry brush to remove most of the marinade, keeping it in reserve, then brown the chicken pieces in the ghee or oil until lightly coloured. Pour off excess oil. Stir water into reserved marinade and pour over the chicken. Cover and cook gently until the chicken is tender (about 25 minutes), stirring and turning occasionally.

Check seasoning and add the chopped coriander before serving.

SERVES 6

Chettinad tomato chicken

½ teaspoon fennel seeds

1 large cinnamon stick

3 cloves

4 cardamom pods, cracked

1½ teaspoons coriander seeds, dry-fried

3 dried red chillies, deseeded

½ teaspoon black peppercorns

250 g freshly grated coconut (or use 200 g desiccated coconut)

½ cup vegetable oil

1 large onion, finely sliced

1-cm piece fresh ginger, grated

4 cloves garlic, crushed

3 star anise

1.25 kg chicken drumsticks

2 teaspoons tomato paste

2 large red tomatoes, deseeded and chopped

1–4 fresh red chillies, deseeded and sliced

salt

fresh lemon or lime juice

Garam Masala (page 18)

chopped fresh coriander

Grind the first 7 ingredients finely, then add the coconut and process to a paste.

Heat the oil in a heavy pan and sauté the onion until well coloured (but not too brown). Add the ginger and garlic and fry for 1–2 minutes, then add the star anise, chicken and tomato paste and cook for 5–6 minutes, stirring frequently. >

Add the coconut spice paste to the pan and cook, stirring, for 1–2 minutes, then add the tomatoes and sliced chillies, and water to barely cover the chicken.

Simmer gently for about 35 minutes, until the chicken is tender. Add salt to taste, and finish the dish with a squeeze of lemon or lime juice and a sprinkle of garam masala. Garnish with the chopped coriander.

SERVES 4–6

Malaysian chicken

1 kg chicken pieces

400 ml coconut milk

1 onion, chopped

1 teaspoon salt

1 large potato, cubed

1 tablespoon hot Malaysian
  curry paste

3 cloves garlic, chopped

1-cm piece fresh ginger,
  chopped

6 shallots, chopped

2 tablespoons ghee or oil

1 teaspoon ground turmeric

1 cinnamon stick

4 cloves

½ teaspoon grated or
  ground nutmeg

1 cup peas

chopped fresh herbs (e.g.
  coriander, basil, mint)

Place chicken pieces in a saucepan with the coconut milk, onion, salt, potato and curry paste, and add water to barely cover the chicken. Bring to the boil then reduce to a simmer.

Grind the garlic, ginger and shallots to a paste, and fry in the ghee or oil for 3–4 minutes in a small pan, stirring frequently. Add the turmeric, cinnamon, cloves and nutmeg. Stir this mixture into the curry and simmer gently for about 15 minutes. Add the peas and cook until soft, by which time the chicken and potato should be very tender. Garnish with fresh herbs.

SERVES 6

Balinese chicken
in creamy spiced sauce

6 tablespoons peanut or
vegetable oil

1 onion, finely sliced

1.5 kg chicken pieces

1 extra onion, very finely
chopped

3 cloves garlic, crushed

2-cm piece fresh galangal,
grated or finely sliced

1 tablespoon ground coriander

1 teaspoon ground cumin

1 teaspoon shrimp paste

1 tablespoon tamarind water

4 candlenuts or 7 macadamias,
crushed to a paste

3 tablespoons kecap manis

2 cups coconut cream

1 teaspoon salt

½ teaspoon chilli flakes

In a frying pan heat 3 tablespoons of the oil and fry the sliced onion until well browned (but do not allow to burn). Lift out and set aside. In the same oil fry the chicken pieces until evenly coloured, then remove.

In a heavy saucepan heat the remaining oil and fry the chopped onion until golden-brown. Add the garlic and galangal, fry briefly and then add the coriander, cumin and shrimp paste and fry, stirring constantly, for 2–3 minutes. >

Add tamarind water, crushed nuts, kecap manis and coconut cream, to the pan, and heat to boiling. Add the chicken, salt and chilli flakes, and simmer for about 30 minutes, until the chicken is tender, stirring and turning occasionally.

Check seasonings before serving.

SERVES 6

Thai green chicken curry

1 cup coconut cream

2–3 teaspoons Thai Green Curry Paste (page 20)

1 stalk lemongrass, slit lengthways

600 g chicken breast, very thinly sliced

2 roma tomatoes

3 kaffir lime leaves or a strip of lime rind (optional)

2 spring onions, chopped

1 tablespoon fish sauce

1 tablespoon fresh lime juice

salt

sugar

a few sprigs fresh basil

In a medium-sized saucepan simmer the coconut cream for 3–4 minutes, until it looks oily, then add the curry paste and lemongrass and cook over medium heat, stirring constantly, until very fragrant. Add 2 cups water and bring to the boil. Reduce heat and simmer for 5–6 minutes.

Cut the tomatoes in half, scoop out the seeds and the fleshy centre, and cut into strips. Stir tomatoes, lime leaves (if using), chicken and spring onions into the sauce. Add fish sauce and lime juice and simmer for 2–3 minutes. Check seasonings, adjusting with salt and sugar. Serve in a bowl, garnished with the basil.

SERVES 6

Sri Lankan chicken with roasted spices

6 dried chillies

3 teaspoons black peppercorns

2½ tablespoons coriander seeds

2 teaspoons cumin seeds

1½ teaspoons black mustard
 seeds

1 stick cinnamon

½ teaspoon ajwain or
 caraway seeds

3 tablespoons oil

6 chicken thigh fillets, halved

1 onion, cut into thin wedges,
 layers separated

2 cups coconut milk

1 teaspoon salt

1 tablespoon tamarind water

12 baby okra

In a pan combine the chillies, peppercorns, coriander, cumin and mustard seeds. Roast over medium heat, stirring and shaking frequently, until dark and aromatic. Transfer to a processor or mortar with the cinnamon and ajwain or caraway. Grind to a fine powder and sift through a fine nylon sieve.

In a larger pan, heat the oil and brown the chicken pieces in two or three batches, then remove to a plate. Reheat the pan and brown the onion. Add the spices and cook, stirring, until fragrant (about 2 minutes). Return chicken to pan and add the coconut milk and salt. Simmer for about 15 minutes, until chicken is almost cooked. Add the tamarind and okra and continue to simmer until both chicken and okra are tender.

SERVES 4–6

Kolivartha chicken

600 g skinless chicken thigh
  fillets, quartered

4 cloves garlic, chopped

1.5-cm piece fresh ginger,
  chopped

1 onion, coarsely chopped

1 large tomato, deseeded and
  chopped

2 tablespoons ghee or oil

½ cup almond meal, or finely
  ground raw cashews

1 teaspoon Garam Masala
  (page 18)

1 tablespoon ground coriander

1 teaspoon ground cumin

½–1 teaspoon chilli powder

½ teaspoon turmeric

2–3 cloves

1½ cups coconut milk

salt

fresh lemon or lime juice

chopped fresh coriander,
  or extra garam masala

Rinse the chicken in cold water, drain well and pat dry with paper towels.

Process or grind the garlic, ginger and onion to a paste. Add the tomato.

Heat the ghee or oil and sauté the chicken pieces until lightly coloured.
Lift out with a slotted spoon and set aside. In the same pan sauté the
tomato mixture for 5–6 minutes, stirring constantly, then add the almond
meal or cashews and the spices and cook, stirring, for 1 minute. >

Return the chicken pieces to the pan, pour in the coconut milk and add salt to taste. Simmer over low heat, uncovered, until chicken is tender and the sauce thick and fragrant (about 18 minutes).

Finish the curry with a squeeze of lemon or lime juice and a sprinkle of chopped coriander or garam masala.

SERVES 6

Jalfraise chicken

1 onion, finely chopped

3 tablespoons ghee or butter

1 teaspoon grated fresh ginger

1 clove garlic, crushed

2 tablespoons ground almonds

1 teaspoon ground turmeric

1 teaspoon mild curry powder

1 teaspoon ground cumin

2 teaspoons ground coriander

4 cloves

4 cardamom pods, cracked

1 cinnamon stick

3 tablespoons natural yoghurt

2 large tomatoes, skinned, deseeded and sliced

500 g chicken breast, cubed

salt and black pepper

⅓ green capsicum, trimmed and finely sliced

1–2 tablespoons slivered almonds, toasted

2–3 tablespoons thick cream (optional)

1 fresh hot red chilli, deseeded and finely sliced

2 hardboiled eggs, sliced

In a medium-sized saucepan fry the onion in the ghee or butter until soft and lightly coloured (about 4 minutes). Add the ginger and garlic and fry another 30 seconds, then add the ground almonds and the spices and fry, stirring frequently, for 2–3 minutes. >

Add to the pan the yoghurt, tomatoes, chicken and ½ cup water, and simmer, stirring often, until the chicken is tender (about 10 minutes). Season to taste with salt and pepper, stir in capsicum strips and slivered almonds, and cook just long enough for the capsicum to soften, stirring often.

Stir in the cream, if using, and transfer to a serving dish. Garnish with chilli shreds and sliced eggs.

SERVES 6

Creamy chicken curry with fruit and nuts

500 g chicken thigh fillets, cut into 1.5-cm cubes

150 g butter

250 g very ripe tomatoes, deseeded and chopped

1 tablespoon tomato paste

¼ teaspoon fenugreek seeds, crushed

½ teaspoon ground hot chilli

4 tablespoons thick cream

2–3 teaspoons fresh lemon juice

sugar

salt and black pepper

1–2 tablespoons chopped fresh coriander

2 hardboiled eggs, cut into wedges

1 tablespoon blanched almonds, toasted

½–¾ cup diced fresh fruit (e.g. mango, pineapple, banana, pear, apple)

Sauté the chicken in the butter until cooked through and lightly coloured (about 6 minutes). Remove with a slotted spoon and keep warm.

Add tomatoes and tomato paste to the pan, and cook for 5 minutes over reasonably high heat, until pulpy. Purée in a food processor (or pass through a sieve) and return to the pan. Add spices and cream, and season to taste with lemon juice, sugar, salt and pepper.

Return chicken to the pan, add the coriander, egg wedges, almonds and fruit, and gently warm through before serving.

SERVES 6

Xacutti chicken in hot and sour coconut curry

1 kg chicken drumsticks

¾ cup desiccated coconut

3–6 dried chillies

1 tablespoon coriander seeds

½ teaspoon cumin seeds

½ teaspoon fenugreek seeds

5 black peppercorns

3 tablespoons ghee or oil

1 onion, grated

4 cloves garlic, crushed

1.5-cm piece fresh ginger, grated

½ teaspoon ground turmeric

4 cloves

1 cinnamon stick

4 cardamom pods, cracked

1 cup coconut milk

salt and black pepper

fresh lemon juice, to taste

With a sharp knife, make several deep slashes across the thickest parts of the chicken drumsticks. Rinse and pat dry with paper towel.

Combine the coconut, chillies, coriander, cumin, fenugreek and peppercorns in a frying pan and dry-fry over medium heat until well browned and very fragrant, making sure the coconut does not burn. Tip immediately into a grinder or mortar and grind to a fine powder.

Wipe out the frying pan, add the ghee or oil and brown the drumsticks, then remove from the pan. Add onion, garlic and ginger and sauté until lightly coloured, then add the previously ground spices, along with the turmeric, cloves, cinnamon and cardamom, and stir over medium heat for 1–2 minutes. >

Return chicken to pan, pour in the coconut milk, add a large pinch of salt and simmer for about 25 minutes, until the chicken is tender and the sauce thick (stir occasionally to prevent sticking). Season to taste with salt and pepper, and a squeeze of lemon juice, and serve.

SERVES 6

Chicken molee

500 g chicken breast or thigh
  fillet, diced

1 large potato, diced

8 curry leaves

3–4 shallots, sliced

4 cloves garlic, sliced

2 green chillies, deseeded
  and sliced

400 ml coconut milk

1 teaspoon ground turmeric

1 tablespoon ground coriander

2 teaspoons ground cumin

1 teaspoon ground white pepper

1 teaspoon salt

fresh lemon juice

2 teaspoons black mustard seeds

ghee or oil

Place the chicken and potato in a heavy saucepan with everything else
except the lemon juice, mustard seeds and ghee or oil. Bring barely to
the boil, then reduce heat and simmer for about 15 minutes, or until the
chicken is tender. Check seasonings and add a squeeze of lemon juice,
to taste.

Fry the mustard seeds in ghee or oil until they pop, and stir into the curry
just before serving.

SERVES 6

Chicken tikka

750 g skinless chicken breast
    or thigh fillets
6 cloves garlic
1 tablespoon fresh lemon juice
1-cm piece fresh ginger, chopped
1 teaspoon ground sweet paprika
1 small onion
1 sprig fresh coriander

3 tablespoons natural yoghurt
1 tablespoon vegetable oil
⅓ teaspoon ground turmeric
¾ teaspoon salt
½ teaspoon sambal ulek
2 teaspoons mild curry paste
1 teaspoon each red and yellow
    food colouring (optional)

Cut the chicken into pieces about 8 cm × 5 cm and place in a shallow dish.
Put remaining ingredients in a food processor, and grind to a smooth paste.
Spread the mixture over the chicken, turning each piece to coat evenly.
Cover and refrigerate for at least 2 hours (or overnight).

Preheat oven to its highest setting.

Place the chicken on a wire rack in an oven tray and cook for about
30 minutes, until tender and the edges flecked black.

Chicken tikka can also be cooked on a barbecue hotplate or grill,
    turning frequently.

SERVES 6

Butter chicken

½ quantity cooked chicken tikka
  (page 110)

150 g butter

400 g canned crushed tomatoes

1 teaspoon ground sweet paprika

1½ teaspoons crushed fresh
  ginger

2 tablespoons chopped fresh
  coriander

2 teaspoons Garam Masala
  (page 18)

2 tablespoons raw cashews,
  finely ground

¼ cup cream

salt

¼ cup sour cream

Cut chicken tikka into bite-sized pieces.

Melt ⅔ of the butter in a saucepan and add the tomatoes, paprika, ginger, coriander, garam masala and cashews. Bring to the boil, then reduce heat and simmer for about 8 minutes, until the tomatoes lose their 'raw' fragrance and are soft and aromatic. Purée in a food processor, or pass through a sieve, and return to the pan.

Add the chicken and cream to the pan, with salt to taste, and warm through. Just before serving, swirl through the remaining butter (cut into cubes) and the sour cream.

SERVES 4

Chicken korma

400 g chicken breast fillets

1 large onion, finely chopped

3 tablespoons ghee or oil

60 g raw cashews or almonds,
  finely ground

1 stick cinnamon

6 cardamom pods, cracked

4 cloves

1 fresh mild red chilli, deseeded
  and sliced

2 cloves garlic, crushed

1-cm piece fresh ginger, grated

1 teaspoon ground coriander

½ teaspoon ground cumin

⅓ teaspoon turmeric

300 ml natural yoghurt

salt and black pepper

Cut the chicken into 1.5-cm cubes and set aside.

Gently sauté the onion in the ghee or oil for about 8 minutes, until well softened but only lightly coloured. Add all the remaining ingredients except the yoghurt, salt and pepper, and stir over a low heat for 1 minute.

Add yoghurt and 1 cup cold water to the pan, and bring to boil. Reduce heat and simmer for 5 minutes. Add chicken and bring almost to the boil, then reduce heat, cover and simmer until chicken is tender (about 25 minutes). Before serving, add salt and pepper to taste.

SERVES 4–6

Chicken with cream

1 kg chicken pieces (or just use drumsticks)

3 tablespoons ghee or oil

2 fresh hot green chillies, deseeded and sliced

5 cloves garlic, chopped

2-cm piece fresh ginger, chopped

8 shallots, chopped

1½ teaspoons salt

½ cup natural yoghurt

⅓ teaspoon ground turmeric

1 teaspoon ground coriander

1 teaspoon ground cumin

1 teaspoon ground sweet paprika

extra salt, and black pepper

⅔ cup cream

Garam Masala (page 18)

Brown the chicken pieces in half the ghee or oil in a large pan. Transfer to a heavy saucepan.

Process or grind the chillies, garlic, ginger and shallots to a paste with the salt. Fry in the remaining oil for about 4 minutes, stirring frequently, until softened and coloured. Add the yoghurt and stir into the chicken. Cook over moderate heat, stirring frequently, until the yoghurt has been absorbed (about 8 minutes).

Sprinkle in the ground spices, add 1½ cups of water and bring to the boil, then reduce heat and simmer for about 20 minutes, partially covered, until the chicken is tender. Season to taste with salt and pepper, stir in the cream and simmer gently until sauce is reduced and creamy.

Sprinkle with garam masala before serving.

SERVES 6

Chicken Madras

500 g chicken thigh fillet

1 tablespoon natural yoghurt

1 fresh red chilli, deseeded
and chopped

2 cloves garlic, crushed

1-cm piece fresh ginger, grated

½ teaspoon salt

½ teaspoon ground cumin

2 onions, very finely chopped

2 tablespoons ghee or oil

3–5 teaspoons Madras curry
paste

1 cup canned crushed tomatoes

2–3 teaspoons tomato paste

black pepper

Garam Masala (page 18)

Cut chicken pieces in half and place in a dish with the yoghurt, chilli, garlic, ginger, salt and cumin. Mix until each piece is coated with the seasonings, then cover and refrigerate for 3–4 hours, or overnight.

In a medium-sized saucepan fry the onions in the ghee or oil until soft and browned (about 8 minutes). Add curry paste and cook for another minute, stirring. Stir in tomatoes and tomato paste, and simmer for 2 minutes over a low heat. Add chicken to the pan with 1 cup water and bring to the boil.

Reduce heat and simmer, partially covered, for about 25 minutes, until chicken is cooked and the sauce thick and aromatic. Check seasonings, then serve in a bowl, sprinkled with garam masala.

SERVES 4–6

Spiced roast chicken

1 × 1.8-kg chicken

4 cloves garlic, crushed

1-cm piece fresh ginger, grated

1½ teaspoons Garam Masala
   (page 18)

1 teaspoon ground hot chilli

1 teaspoon salt

1 tablespoon fresh lemon juice

3 tablespoons natural yoghurt

⅓ teaspoon powdered saffron

2 teaspoons garam masala, extra

chopped fresh coriander,
   for garnish

SPICY BASTE

1 large onion, very finely chopped

3 cloves garlic, crushed

1.5-cm piece fresh ginger, grated

4 tablespoons ghee or oil

6 cloves

8 black peppercorns

4 cardamom pods, cracked

1 cinnamon stick

1 cup natural yoghurt

Rinse the chicken inside and out, drain well and dry with paper towels. Make a seasoning paste by combining the garlic, ginger, garam masala, ground chilli, salt, lemon juice and yoghurt. Paint paste in the cavity of the chicken, then spread over the outside. Set in a dish, cover and leave for 2–3 hours to marinate.

Preheat oven to 180°. >

To make the spicy baste, brown the onion, garlic and ginger in the ghee or oil. Add the spices and yoghurt, and simmer for about 2 minutes, until fragrant and well blended.

Place the chicken in an oven dish. Spread the spicy baste evenly over, cover, and cook in oven for about 30 minutes. Every 10 minutes, uncover chicken and baste with the pan juices.

To complete the cooking, uncover chicken, increase oven temperature to 210 °C and allow to brown on the top. Stir the saffron into 2 tablespoons of water and sprinkle over the chicken, together with the garam masala. Serve garnished with the chopped coriander.

SERVES 6–8

Red chicken and bamboo curry

400 ml coconut cream

1–3 teaspoons Thai Red Curry Paste (page 19)

300-g chicken breast, thinly sliced

150 g shredded bamboo shoots

1½ tablespoons fish sauce

½ teaspoon sugar

3 kaffir lime leaves (optional)

1 fresh hot red chilli, deseeded
    and shredded

salt

fresh basil leaves

Place ½ cup of the coconut cream in a saucepan and bring to the boil. Simmer, stirring constantly, until oil separates (about 3 minutes), then add the curry paste and cook briefly. Stir in the remaining coconut cream and simmer for 2 minutes, stirring occasionally.

Add the chicken and bamboo shoots and cook for 1 minute, then add the fish sauce, sugar, lime leaves (if using) and chilli, and simmer a further 3 minutes. Check seasonings, adding salt if needed. Stir in basil leaves before serving.

SERVES 4

Kukul mas curry
(Sri Lankan chicken curry)

2 tablespoons curry powder

6 skinless chicken thigh fillets

salt

2 teaspoons ground sweet
  paprika

3 tablespoons oil

1 onion, chopped

1-cm piece fresh ginger, finely
  chopped

3 cloves garlic, finely chopped

½ stalk lemongrass, finely
  chopped

1-2 fresh hot green chillies,
  slit and deseeded

2 tomatoes, deseeded and
  chopped

1 stick cinnamon

5 cloves

4 cardamom pods, cracked

1 cup coconut cream

fresh lemon or lime juice

chopped fresh herbs
  (e.g. coriander, mint, basil)

Dry-fry curry powder in a small pan until fragrant. Season the chicken pieces with salt, then rub in the curry powder and paprika. Cover, and marinate in the refrigerator for 4–5 hours, or overnight.

Heat the oil in a heavy pan and fry the onion over medium heat for about 6 minutes, until soft and lightly coloured. Add the ginger, garlic, lemongrass and chillies and fry 1 minute, stirring. Add the chicken, increase heat a little and add the tomatoes, cinnamon, cloves and cardamom. Turn the chicken several times and stir to prevent the onions sticking.

When chicken is lightly coloured, pour in the coconut cream and add ½ cup water, plus salt to taste. When sauce is almost boiling, reduce heat and simmer for about 20 minutes until the chicken is tender and the sauce well reduced.

Just before serving, add a squeeze of lemon or lime juice and stir in the chopped herbs.

SERVES 6

Thai green duck curry

1 × 1.8 kg–2 kg duck

2 cups coconut cream

1–1½ tablespoons Thai Green
Curry Paste (page 20)

12 small pickling onions

2 cups coconut milk

4 kaffir lime leaves (optional)

salt and fish sauce to taste

2 teaspoons sugar

3 roma tomatoes

fresh lime juice

small bunch fresh basil,
leaves picked

zest of 1 lime, cut into
matchstick slices

Cut the duck into serving portions and place in a colander. Rinse in cold water and drain very well.

In a wok or large saucepan heat the coconut cream for about 8 minutes, stirring frequently, until it has a shimmer of oil on the surface. Stir in the curry paste and cook, stirring often, for about 5 minutes. Add the duck and cook in the thick and spicy seasoning for about 10 minutes, turning often and taking care the paste does not stick.

Add onions and coconut milk to pan with, if needed, enough to water to almost cover the duck. Bring to the boil, reduce heat and simmer for 20 minutes. Add lime leaves (if using), salt and fish sauce to taste, and the sugar. Continue to cook until the duck is tender (about 20 minutes). >

Cut the tomatoes lengthways in half and scoop out the seeds and fleshy centres. Cut into long strips. Add tomatoes to the curry and cook for 1–2 minutes. Add a generous squeeze of lime juice, stir in the basil leaves, and sprinkle with the lime zest before serving.

SERVES 6–8

Quick Thai red duck curry with grape tomatoes

½ Chinese roast duck

2–4 teaspoons Thai Red
Curry Paste (page 19)

2 tablespoons oil

400 ml coconut milk

½ punnet yellow grape
tomatoes, halved

1½ tablespoons fish sauce

1 tablespoon palm sugar
or soft brown sugar

12 fresh Thai basil leaves

Remove duck meat from the bones and cut into bite-sized pieces.
Set aside.

In a medium-sized saucepan fry the curry paste in oil for 2 minutes, stirring constantly. Add the coconut milk and ½ cup water and bring almost to the boil. Reduce heat and simmer gently for about 6 minutes. Add the duck, tomatoes, fish sauce, sugar and basil leaves, and heat gently for about 3 minutes before serving.

SERVES 4

Roast duck yellow curry

350 g duck breast fillet

3 cloves garlic

4 red or brown shallots

2-cm piece fresh ginger, chopped

½ stalk lemongrass, chopped

1 teaspoon shrimp paste

2 teaspoons ground turmeric

1 teaspoon cumin seeds

2 teaspoons coriander seeds

2–3 dried red chillies

1 cup coconut cream

3 kaffir lime leaves

2 fresh mild red chillies, slit and deseeded

30 g sliced bamboo shoots

2–3 teaspoons fish sauce

5–6 cherry tomatoes, cut in half

fresh Thai basil leaves

Preheat oven to very hot.

Heat a non-stick pan with no oil and put in the duck breasts, skin-side down. Cook for 2 minutes on each side over high heat. Pour off the oil that has been drawn out. Transfer the pan to preheated oven for 10 minutes, then remove and set aside to rest.

Process or grind the garlic, shallots, ginger, lemongrass, shrimp paste and turmeric to a smooth paste.

In a small dry pan roast the cumin and coriander seeds with the dried chillies, and when very aromatic tip into a spice grinder and grind finely.

Bring the coconut cream to the boil in a medium-sized saucepan and simmer for about 4 minutes, stirring frequently, until it is oily on the surface and has begun to separate. Add the curry paste and cook for 2 minutes, then add ground spices and continue to simmer until the sauce is well blended and aromatic. Add ½ cup cold water and stir in lime leaves, fresh chillies, bamboo shoots and fish sauce, and simmer 2–3 minutes.

Slice the duck and add to the curry with the tomatoes. Add a little extra water if the sauce seems too thick. Simmer just long enough for the duck and tomatoes to heat through, then stir in basil leaves and serve.

SERVES 4

Duck rendang

1 × 2-kg duck
3 cloves garlic, chopped
1-cm piece fresh ginger, chopped
1½ teaspoons salt
800 ml coconut cream
1 large onion, finely chopped
2.5-cm extra piece fresh ginger
   or galangal, chopped

1 stalk lemongrass, slit
   lengthways
2 bay leaves
2–3 teaspoons sambal ulek
1½ teaspoons ground turmeric
1 tablespoon tamarind water
salt and black pepper

Cut the duck into serving pieces. Crush the garlic, ginger and salt to a paste and mix with 3 tablespoons of the coconut cream. Place the duck pieces in a shallow dish, add the seasoning paste and stir the pieces around until evenly coated. Cover and set aside.

In a large saucepan bring the remaining coconut cream to the boil, adding the onion, extra ginger, lemongrass, bay leaves, sambal ulek and turmeric. Add 3 cups of water and simmer for about 20 minutes, until very fragrant and partially reduced.

Add the duck, any remaining marinade and the tamarind water, and simmer gently stirring from time to time, for about 1½ hours. Before serving, check seasonings, adding salt and pepper if needed.

SERVES 6–8

Duck vindaloo

5 dried chillies

1½ tablespoons coriander seeds

2 teaspoons cumin seeds

1 teaspoon fenugreek seeds

½ teaspoon black mustard seeds

½ teaspoon black peppercorns

¾ teaspoon ground turmeric

1½ teaspoons salt

3 tablespoons white vinegar

1 tablespoon tamarind water

1 × 1.5–2-kg duck

3 tablespoons ghee

2 onions, very finely chopped

8 cloves garlic, crushed

2-cm piece fresh ginger, grated

3 fresh green chillies, deseeded
and finely chopped

salt

To make the vindaloo paste, roast the chillies, coriander, cumin, fenugreek and mustard seeds in a dry pan with the peppercorns until very aromatic (about 5 minutes), stirring frequently. Process or grind to a powder, then mix to a paste with the turmeric, salt, vinegar and tamarind water, adding a little water or oil if needed.

To make the curry, rinse and drain the duck and cut into serving pieces. Heat the ghee in a large pan and brown the onions for about 8 minutes, until well browned. Add the garlic, ginger, chillies and 3 tablespoons of the prepared vindaloo paste, and fry for 3–4 minutes over medium heat, stirring frequently.

Add the duck pieces and cook for about 5 minutes, turning frequently and scraping the bottom of the pan to make sure
it doesn't stick.

Add water to not quite cover the duck, cover the pan tightly and when the water comes almost to the boil reduce the heat and simmer gently until duck is very tender (about 40 minutes). If necessary, remove the lid half way through cooking, so the sauce reduces. Season to taste with salt in the last few minutes.

SERVES 6–8

Javanese spicy duck curry

1.8 kg duck portions

2 onions, roughly chopped

6 cloves garlic, chopped

3 fresh green chillies, deseeded
and halved

1 stalk lemongrass, roughly
chopped

1.5-cm piece fresh ginger,
chopped

3 tablespoons peanut
or vegetable oil

1.5-cm piece fresh galangal,
sliced

3 cups coconut milk

1½ teaspoons salt

1 tablespoon tamarind water

sugar

chopped fresh mint or basil

Rinse the duck, drain well and place in a deep saucepan. Grind the onion, garlic, chillies, lemongrass and ginger to a paste with half the oil.

Heat remaining oil in a saucepan and fry the paste for about 8 minutes, stirring frequently. Add galangal and coconut milk, and bring barely to the boil. Pour over the duck, add salt and cook, stirring frequently, over medium heat until duck is very tender and the sauce well reduced (30–40 minutes). Add tamarind water and simmer briefly. Adjust seasonings with extra salt and sugar if needed. Stir in chopped herbs just before serving.

SERVES 8

Indonesian chicken livers

500 g chicken livers

¼ cup vegetable oil

1 large onion, finely chopped

2 garlic cloves, crushed

1-cm piece fresh ginger, finely chopped

2–4 fresh red chillies, deseeded and thinly sliced

1 stalk lemongrass, slit lengthways

12 candlenuts or 18 macadamia nuts, crushed

1½ cups thin coconut milk

½ teaspoon salt

palm sugar

fresh lemon juice

crisp-fried onion

Rinse the livers in cold water and drain well. Trim and cut in half. Fry in the oil until no pink shows. Remove with a slotted spoon and set aside.

In the same oil sauté the onion and garlic until soft and golden. Add the ginger, chillies, lemongrass, crushed nuts, coconut milk and salt. Bring barely to the boil, then reduce heat and simmer for 5 minutes.

Return livers to the pan and cook gently until tender (about 8 minutes). Season to taste with extra salt, sugar and lemon juice, and pour into a serving bowl. Sprinkle with crisp-fried onion flakes.

SERVES 4–6

Beef, lamb and pork

The consumption of beef or pork is prohibited on religious grounds in many parts of Asia and Southeast Asia, so lamb (used interchangeably with mutton and goat) is therefore the predominant meat used for curries.

Many beef curries originated from recipes that used buffalo meat. Beef marries superbly with intense curry spicing and strong, tangy sauces. Lamb is used in all sorts of ways: mashed into koftas, threaded onto skewers, diced finely or chunky into curries with creamy coconut or yoghurt sauces, with herb sauces, with spiced sauces containing lentils and browned onions, with eggplants and pumpkin, and with fruit and nuts. Pork, similarly, is as compatible with the searing heat of a vindaloo as it is with the complex seasonings of Thailand.

Indonesian dry beef curry

1 kg stewing beef

2 cups coconut milk

1 cup water

1 medium-sized onion, finely chopped

3-cm piece fresh ginger, chopped

1 stalk lemongrass, slit lengthways

1 stick cinnamon

6 cloves

5 cardamom pods, cracked

3 tablespoons vegetable oil

4 tablespoons desiccated coconut

1½ tablespoons ground coriander

2 teaspoons ground cumin

½ teaspoon black peppercorns

2 extra onions, finely sliced

1 tablespoon tamarind water

2 teaspoons palm sugar

salt

Cut the beef into 4-cm cubes and place in a heavy saucepan. Add the coconut milk, water, onion, ginger, lemongrass, cinnamon, cloves and cardamom. Bring to the boil, then reduce heat and simmer gently.

Heat half the oil in a pan and brown the coconut, coriander, cumin and peppercorns. Grind finely and add to the pan with the beef. Heat remaining oil and fry the extra onions until browned. Stir into the curry, and add tamarind water and sugar, and salt to taste. Cook for at least 1¼ hours, until the meat is tender and liquid had reduced to a thick paste.

SERVES 6

Madras beef curry

½ cup desiccated coconut

2–3 fresh hot red chillies, deseeded and roughly chopped

1-cm piece fresh ginger, chopped

5–6 cloves garlic, chopped

1 tablespoon ground coriander

1½ teaspoons ground cumin

2-3 teaspoons ground sweet paprika

1 cinnamon stick

4 cloves

½ teaspoon peppercorns

¾ cup coconut cream

1 kg stewing beef, cut into 4-cm pieces

2 large onions, finely chopped

3 tablespoons ghee or oil

4 roma tomatoes, deseeded and chopped

In a mortar or food processor, grind the coconut, chillies, ginger, garlic and ground spices to a paste. Add the cinnamon, cloves, peppercorns and coconut cream, and combine well. Stir the meat into this marinade and set aside.

In a large saucepan with a heavy base cook the onions in the ghee or oil over medium heat until softened and well browned (8–10 minutes). Add the meat and marinade, and stir over medium-high heat for about 5 minutes.

To the meat in the pan add the tomatoes, water to cover, and salt to taste, and bring to the boil. Reduce heat to a simmer and cook gently for about 1¼ hours, until meat is very tender and sauce well reduced.

SERVES 6

A beef curry from Sumatra

800 g stewing beef, cut into
  2-cm cubes

3 tablespoons vegetable oil

1 large onion, finely chopped

2 cups coconut milk

3 cloves garlic, finely chopped

1-cm piece fresh ginger, finely
  chopped

1 stalk lemongrass, slit
  lengthways

1 teaspoon shrimp paste

1–2 teaspoons sambal ulek

1 teaspoon ground turmeric

2 teaspoons palm sugar

salt

12 baby okra

a handful water spinach
  (kangkong) leaves

tamarind water or fresh
  lime juice

Brown the beef, in batches, in the oil. Remove and set aside. In the same pan fry the onion until well coloured, then add the coconut milk and bring to a rapid boil. Simmer for 2 minutes, then add the garlic, ginger, lemongrass, shrimp and chilli pastes, and turmeric, and simmer for 5 minutes.

Return the meat to the pan, add the sugar and salt to taste and cook for about 50 minutes, until the meat is almost tender. Add the okra and water spinach, and cook for 5–6 minutes. Check seasonings, adding a splash of tamarind water or a squeeze of fresh lime juice, to taste.

SERVES 6

Thai beef and long-bean curry

800 g stewing beef, cut into
  2-cm cubes

3 cups coconut milk

1 onion, finely chopped

2 tablespoons oil

1½ tablespoons Thai Red
  Curry Paste (page 19)

1 stalk lemongrass, slit
  lengthways

1–2 fresh mild red chillies,
  deseeded and sliced

6 snake beans or 12 green beans,
  cut into 5-cm lengths

2 tablespoons fish sauce

1 tablespoon fresh lime juice

salt

2 teaspoons palm sugar or soft
  brown sugar

Simmer the beef in the coconut milk for 40 minutes.

Meanwhile, lightly brown the onion in the oil and add ½ cup of the beef
cooking liquid, plus the curry paste, lemongrass and chillies, and cook over
high heat, stirring continually, until very fragrant (about 4 minutes). Pour
over the beef and continue to simmer until almost tender (30–40 minutes).

Add the beans, fish sauce and lime juice to the curry, with sugar and salt
to taste and simmer until the meat and beans are well cooked (about
8 minutes).

SERVES 6

Sri Lankan meatballs (frikkadels)

500 g finely minced beef

½ cup desiccated coconut

½ teaspoon fresh crushed garlic

2 tablespoons grated onion

2 teaspoons finely chopped fresh
dill or mint

1 tablespoon fresh lemon juice

½ teaspoon salt

½ teaspoon ground black
pepper

1 egg, well beaten

1 cup dry breadcrumbs

2–3 tablespoons ghee or oil

In a bowl knead together the beef, coconut, garlic, onion, dill or mint, lemon juice, salt and pepper until smooth. With wet hands, form into 24 small balls.

Dip balls into beaten egg and coat with the breadcrumbs. Heat ghee or oil in a shallow pan over medium heat and fry the meatballs until well browned and cooked through (about 3 minutes). Remove with a slotted spoon and drain on paper towels.

Serve as an appetiser with chutney or a hot sambal.

MAKES 24

Thai masaman beef and potato curry

1 kg stewing beef, cut into
   2-cm cubes

3½ cups thin coconut milk

1 cup chopped roasted peanuts

1½ tablespoons fish sauce

4–8 dried red chillies

2 tablespoons coriander seeds

6 black peppercorns

1 teaspoon caraway seeds

1 stick cinnamon

3 cardamom pods, cracked

8 cloves

2 potatoes, cut into 2-cm cubes

1 stalk lemongrass, chopped

2-cm piece fresh ginger,
   chopped

4 cloves garlic, chopped

1 teaspoon salt

8 shallots, finely sliced

vegetable oil

½ teaspoon shrimp paste

2–3 teaspoons palm sugar
   or soft brown sugar

1 tablespoon tamarind water

extra fish sauce

fresh curry leaves and chopped
   fresh green chillies

Place the beef in a saucepan with the coconut milk, peanuts and fish sauce. Bring to boil, then reduce the heat and simmer for about 1 hour, until meat is almost tender. >

In a dry pan roast the chillies, coriander, peppercorns and caraway for about 2 minutes, until aromatic. Process or grind to a fine powder, then add to the meat with the cinnamon, cardamom and cloves, together with the cubed potatoes.

In a mortar or processor grind the lemongrass, ginger, garlic and salt to a smooth paste.

In a small pan fry the shallots in the oil, and when lightly coloured add the shrimp paste and prepared lemongrass paste, and fry for 2–3 minutes over medium heat until very aromatic. Stir this mixture into the meat and continue cooking until meat and potatoes are tender (about 20 minutes).

Dilute the sugar in ⅓ cup water and pour over the meat. Add the tamarind water and simmer for a further 2–3 minutes, stirring. Check seasonings, and add fish sauce to taste. Garnish with curry leaves and chopped green chillies before serving.

SERVES 6–8

Lamb dopiaza

1 kg onions, peeled

5 cloves garlic, crushed

1½ teaspoons crushed
fresh ginger

2 teaspoons ground mild
red paprika

1–2 fresh red chillies, deseeded
and chopped

3 tablespoons finely chopped
fresh coriander (leaves and
some stems)

2 tablespoons coriander seeds

2 teaspoons cumin seeds

⅓ cup natural yoghurt

⅓ cup ghee

2 tablespoons vegetable oil

1.5 kg lamb shoulder or leg,
cubed

8 cardamom pods, cracked

1 teaspoon Garam Masala
(page 18)

Finely slice half the onion and set aside. Coarsely chop the remainder and place in a food processor or mortar. Grind to a paste with the garlic, ginger, paprika, chillies, and fresh coriander.

Separately grind the coriander and cumin seeds to a fine powder. Stir into the onion paste, add the yoghurt and mix well. If desired, pass the mixture through a fine nylon sieve, to give a smooth paste.

Heat the ghee and oil in a large pan and fry the sliced onions until evenly browned. They should be well coloured, but do not allow them to burn. Remove with a slotted spoon and set aside. Add the meat, in batches, to the remaining oil, frying until lightly browned. Remove and set aside. >

Fry the yoghurt–onion mixture in the same pan for 3–5 minutes, until very aromatic, then return the meat and add enough water to barely cover, and the cardamom pods. Simmer over low heat for about 30 minutes, until the meat is almost tender. Add the browned onions and garam masala, and continue to cook very gently for a further 15 minutes.

Dopiaza is a rich onion-based sauce. You can buy this sauce ready-made in Indian food stores and some supermarkets, but the results are more flavourful if you make your own.

SERVES 8

Lamb and jackfruit
in creamy curry sauce

250 g lean lamb (or beef), cubed

1 stalk lemongrass, split lengthways

3-cm piece fresh ginger, chopped

¼ cup finely chopped shallots

1 clove garlic, crushed

1 fresh red chilli, deseeded and finely chopped

1 teaspoon ground turmeric

2 teaspoons shrimp paste

2 tablespoons vegetable oil

1 cup coconut cream

200 g jackfruit (or use barely ripe pineapple), cubed

tamarind water or fresh lemon juice

sugar

salt and black pepper

Place meat in a saucepan with the lemongrass and ginger. Add salted water to barely cover, and simmer for 20 minutes.

Grind the shallots, garlic and chilli in a food processor or mortar, then add turmeric and shrimp paste. Fry this paste in oil for 2–3 minutes. Add coconut cream and bring almost to the boil, then reduce heat and simmer gently for 3–4 minutes.

Use a slotted spoon to transfer meat to the coconut sauce, add the jackfruit (or pineapple) and strain in meat-poaching liquid to not quite cover the meat. Simmer gently until meat is tender (about 15 minutes). Adjust flavours with tamarind water or lemon juice, and sugar, salt and pepper.

SERVES 4–6

Vindaloo of beef rib fingers

2 tablespoons ground coriander

1 tablespoon ground cumin

1 tablespoon crushed fresh garlic

2 teaspoons grated fresh ginger

1 large onion, grated

½ cup white vinegar

2 teaspoons salt

1 kg beef rib fingers, cut into
   3-cm pieces

3 tablespoons ghee or oil

6 cloves

4 cardamom pods, cracked

2 bay leaves

2–6 dried red chillies, deseeded

2 teaspoons black peppercorns

beef stock (optional)

In a bowl combine the coriander, cumin, garlic, ginger, juice from the grated onion (save the solids), vinegar and salt. Place meat in a shallow dish and pour marinade over, then turn and knead the meat until each piece is evenly covered. Cover, and refrigerate for at least 4 hours.

Tip marinated meat into a colander and leave to drain for 10 minutes, reserving the liquid. In a saucepan heat the ghee or oil and fry meat in batches until well browned. Set aside. Fry onion solids for 2–3 minutes, then add the cloves, cardamom, bay leaves, chillies and peppercorns, and the reserved marinade. Add water or beef stock to barely cover, and bring to the boil. Reduce heat and simmer very gently for about 1½ hours, until the meat is so tender it is falling apart. Check seasonings, adding more salt if needed.

SERVES 8

Seekh kebabs

1 teaspoon ground cumin

1 teaspoon ground coriander

1½ tablespoons chickpea flour (besan)

600 g boneless lamb, diced

1½ teaspoons grated fresh ginger

1 teaspoon crushed garlic

pinch of ground cloves

1 cardamom pod, peeled and seeds ground

¼ cup natural yoghurt

1 teaspoon salt

2 tablespoons ghee or oil

1 small white or red onion, sliced

lime wedges

In a small dry pan toast the cumin, coriander and chickpea flour for about 2 minutes over medium heat, until fragrant. Tip into the bowl of a food processor and add the lamb, ginger, garlic, spices, yoghurt and salt. Process to a smooth paste. With wet hands form lamb mixture into balls. Thread three or four onto a metal skewer, until all balls have been used.

Heat a grill, hotplate or barbecue. Brush kebabs with melted ghee or oil, and grill, turning frequently, for about 5 minutes. Serve hot with onion slices and lime wedges.

SERVES 4–6

Spiced lamb (gulai kambing)

650 g lean lamb, cut into
   1.5-cm cubes

salt and black pepper

3 tablespoons vegetable oil

1 onion, thinly sliced

1 cup chopped onions, extra

2 tablespoons finely chopped
   garlic

2 tablespoons finely chopped
   fresh ginger

2 teaspoons ground turmeric

1 teaspoon shrimp paste

2 teaspoons palm sugar
   or soft brown sugar

1–2 fresh red chillies, deseeded
   and sliced

400 g coconut milk

fresh coriander or basil leaves

Season the lamb with salt and pepper. Heat the oil in a large pan and
brown the lamb in batches, then remove and set aside.

Brown the sliced onion in the same pan, and set aside with the meat.
Then sauté the chopped onion, garlic and ginger for 6 minutes, stirring
frequently. Add turmeric, shrimp paste and sugar, and sauté briefly, then
add the chillies and coconut milk.

Return the lamb to the pan and simmer gently until lamb is very tender and
oil floats on the surface of the curry (about 40 minutes). Season to taste
with salt and pepper, and stir in the herbs just before serving.

SERVES 6–8

Lamb saag
(lamb and spinach curry)

750 g lean lamb, cubed

2 tablespoons ghee or butter

1 fresh green chilli, deseeded
and finely chopped

2 cloves garlic, crushed

1-cm piece fresh ginger, grated

1 teaspoon salt

1½ teaspoons ground coriander

2 cardamom pods, cracked

1 small cinnamon stick

400 g frozen chopped spinach,
defrosted

½–¾ cup pouring cream

½ teaspoon grated nutmeg

Working in batches, brown the lamb in the ghee or butter and remove
with a slotted spoon. Set aside on a plate.

Add the chilli, garlic and ginger to the pan and cook for 40 seconds, then
return the lamb and add the salt, coriander, cardamom and cinnamon, plus
1 cup water. Simmer for about 30 minutes, until the lamb is tender and
has absorbed the liquid. If liquid diminishes too quickly, add a little more,
as needed.

Add the spinach, cream and nutmeg to the pan and simmer gently until
heated through and the flavours well blended (about 6 minutes), adding
a little water if sauce becomes too dry. Check seasoning and serve.

SERVES 6

Rogan josh

800 g boneless lamb, cut into 3-cm cubes

2–3 tablespoons ghee or oil

4 cloves

4 cardamom pods, cracked

1 cinnamon stick

6 black peppercorns

2 bay leaves

1 medium-sized onion, finely chopped

4 cloves garlic, finely chopped

2-cm piece fresh ginger, finely chopped

1–2 fresh hot green chillies, deseeded and chopped

3 teaspoons ground coriander

1 teaspoon ground cumin

½ teaspoon ground ginger

1 teaspoon Kashmiri (mild) chilli powder

1 tablespoon tomato paste

½ cup natural yoghurt or sour cream

Brown lamb in batches in the ghee or oil. Remove with a slotted spoon and set aside.

Add the whole spices to the pan and fry for 1 minute, stirring. Add the onion and fry, stirring frequently, until well browned, then reduce heat and add garlic, ginger, chillies, ground spices and tomato paste. Mix well and cook over low heat for 30 seconds, then add 1 tablespoon of the yoghurt or sour cream and stir well. >

Add the remaining yoghurt or sour cream and stir for another 1–2 minutes, until the sauce is well blended and fragrant. Return the meat and any liquid it has released, add water barely to cover and bring to the boil. Simmer, uncovered, for about 40 minutes until the meat is tender and the sauce well reduced. Add salt to taste before serving.

SERVES 6

Lamb korma

2 tablespoons ghee

1 large onion, thinly sliced

750 g boneless lamb, cubed

½ teaspoon ground chilli

¾ teaspoon salt

1½ teaspoons ground coriander

4 cloves garlic, crushed

2 teaspoons grated fresh ginger

1 cup natural yoghurt

½–¾ cup water

2 tablespoons thick cream

2 tablespoons flaked almonds

½–1 teaspoon rosewater

Heat the ghee in a frying pan and cook the onion until lightly browned (about 5 minutes). Remove with a slotted spoon and set aside.

Lightly brown the lamb in the same oil, then return the cooked onion, add the spices, garlic and ginger, and stir over medium heat for 2–3 minutes. Add the yoghurt and cook gently, stirring frequently, until most of the liquid has boiled away, then add the water, cover and simmer for about 20 minutes, until the meat is tender. Stir in cream, almonds and rosewater, and warm through.

SERVES 4–6

Lamb and pumpkin curry

1 large onion, halved

3 tablespoons ghee, oil or butter

3 cloves garlic, crushed

1.5-cm piece fresh ginger, grated

500 g boneless lamb, diced

1 teaspoon ground turmeric

2 teaspoons Garam Masala
(page 18)

½ teaspoon crushed fennel
seeds

250 g pumpkin, peeled
and cubed

2 fresh red chillies, deseeded
and sliced

1 bay leaf

salt and black pepper

½ green capsicum, trimmed
and diced

chopped fresh coriander
or mint leaves

Finely slice half the onion, and chop the remainder very finely. Fry the sliced onion in the ghee, oil or butter over medium heat, until very well coloured (about 5 minutes), stirring frequently. Lift out and set aside.

Add the chopped onion, garlic and ginger to the pan and fry until lightly browned. Add the lamb, turmeric, garam masala and fennel seeds with enough water to cover. Bring to the boil, reduce heat and simmer for about 20 minutes, until the lamb is almost tender. >

Add the pumpkin, chillies, bay leaf and salt and pepper to taste, and simmer another 12 minutes. Drop in the chopped capsicum and fried onion slices, and continue to simmer until tender. Check and adjust seasonings, and stir in coriander or mint before serving.

SERVES 4–6

Curried meatballs

1.5 kg shank end of a leg of lamb
   or mutton, on the bone

1 small onion, very finely
   chopped

1-cm piece fresh ginger, grated

salt and black pepper

2 teaspoons Garam Masala
   (page 18)

chickpea flour (besan)

oil for deep-frying

2 medium-sized onions

5 cloves

1 cinnamon stick

1 tablespoon coriander seeds

2 dried red chillies

large pinch of asafoetida

1 teaspoon ground ginger

2 tablespoons ghee

4 cloves garlic, chopped

2 tomatoes, deseeded and
   crushed

pinch of saffron threads

chopped fresh coriander
   or mint leaves

To make the meatballs, use a boning knife to trim the meat from the bone
and cut into rough chunks. Reserve the bone. In batches, chop meat to a
paste in a food processor (or pass through a mincer). Grind or mince the
onion and ginger. >

In a bowl combine the minced lamb, onion, ginger, salt, pepper, and garam masala, and knead until thoroughly mixed and smooth. Cover and set aside.

To make sauce, quarter one of the onions, and chop the other very finely. Place the lamb bone in a large saucepan with the quartered onion and the cloves and cinnamon stick. Add water to cover, bring to the boil, skim, reduce heat and simmer for about 30 minutes to achieve a rich-flavoured lamb stock. Strain and set aside.

In a dry pan roast the coriander seeds and chillies and grind to a fine powder. Mix in the asafoetida and ginger.

Fry the chopped onion in ghee until very well browned (be careful it does not burn). Add the garlic and roasted spices, fry briefly, then add the tomatoes and 2 cups of the prepared stock. Bring to the boil, and simmer while you prepare the meatballs.

With wet hands, form the meat mixture into balls, and coat lightly in chickpea flour. Heat oil for deep-frying, and fry the meatballs in batches until very well browned. As each batch is cooked, transfer to the simmering sauce.

Infuse the saffron in ½ cup of the hot stock, and when bright yellow pour it into the pot. Check seasonings, adding salt and pepper to taste, and stir in chopped herbs before serving.

SERVES 6

Mild pork curry

750 g lean pork, cubed

¼ cup mild curry paste (or use 2½ tablespoons mild curry powder)

2 tablespoons fish sauce

½ cup finely chopped shallots

1 tablespoon finely chopped fresh ginger

2 teaspoons finely chopped garlic

vegetable oil

1 piece cassia bark

4 curry leaves (optional)

3 cups coconut milk

salt and black pepper

In a bowl season the pork with the curry paste or powder and the fish sauce, then mix in the shallots, ginger and garlic. Cover and refrigerate for 2–3 hours.

Heat a large nonstick pan and add 2–3 tablespoons of vegetable oil. Brown the pork in batches until evenly coloured, then return all the pork to the pan and add the remaining ingredients. Bring to the boil, then reduce heat and simmer for about 40 minutes, until the pork is tender and the sauce well reduced.

SERVES 4–6

Keema mattar
(minced lamb with peas)

3 tablespoons ghee or oil

3 cloves

1 cinnamon stick

8 black peppercorns

1 medium-sized onion, finely
chopped

2 cloves garlic, chopped

1-cm piece fresh ginger,
chopped

400 g minced lamb

1–2 fresh chillies, deseeded and
chopped

½ teaspoon ground turmeric

1 teaspoon Garam Masala
(page 18)

1 teaspoon ground cumin

1 cup canned crushed tomatoes

1 cup frozen peas

salt

lemon juice

chopped fresh coriander
or mint leaves

Heat the ghee or oil in a saucepan over medium heat and fry the cloves,
cinnamon and peppercorns for about 30 seconds. Add the onion and fry,
stirring frequently, until lightly browned.

Add the garlic, ginger and lamb to the pan and increase the heat, stirring
for 2–3 minutes until the meat is lightly coloured. Still on high heat, add the
chillies and spices and stir for a few seconds. Add the tomatoes, bring to
the boil, then reduce heat and simmer for 2 minutes.

Add the peas and 1 cup water and simmer until peas are tender and the liquid well reduced (about 10 minutes). Season to taste with salt and lemon juice, and stir in chopped coriander or mint before serving.

SERVES 4 – 6

Lamb koftas in a mild curry

KOFTAS

1 large onion, chopped

3 cloves garlic, chopped

1½ teaspoons salt

1 tablespoon Garam Masala
(page 18)

½ teaspoon ground cinnamon

3–4 sprigs fresh coriander or
mint

1 kg minced lamb

peanut or vegetable oil for
deep-frying

CURRY SAUCE

2 large onions, chopped

4 garlic cloves, chopped

2-cm piece fresh ginger,
chopped

1½ tablespoons coriander seeds

1 teaspoon cumin seeds

2 dried red chillies

3 cloves

2 cardamom pods, cracked

1 cinnamon stick

4 tablespoons ghee

1 cup canned crushed tomatoes

2 teaspoons ground sweet
paprika

½ cup sultanas

1 cup natural yoghurt
or sour cream

salt

thick cream

extra garam masala

chopped fresh coriander
or mint leaves

flaked almonds, toasted

First, make the koftas. Process the onion and garlic with the spices
and herbs until reasonably smooth. Remove half and set aside. >

Add half the meat to the processor and grind to a smooth paste. Remove. Process reserved onion paste and remaining meat to a smooth paste.

Knead the two meat batches together in a large bowl, then with wet hands shape into balls the size of walnuts, and flatten slightly. Heat oil to medium-hot, and fry the meatballs in batches, until well-browned (about 3 minutes). Remove with a slotted spoon and set aside.

To prepare the sauce, process the onions, garlic and ginger to a paste in a food processor and set aside. In a dry pan roast the coriander and cumin seeds with the dried chillies over medium heat until fragrant (about 2 minutes). Trip into a spice grinder and grind to a fine powder. Add the cloves, cardamom and cinnamon and set aside.

In a saucepan with a heavy base, heat the ghee and fry the onion paste for about 8 minutes, until lightly coloured. Add the prepared spices and cook a further 2 minutes, stirring, then add the tomatoes and paprika and simmer for 3–4 minutes. Add 1 cup water and the sultanas, bring briskly to the boil, then reduce heat and simmer for 3–4 minutes. Stir in the yoghurt or sour cream, and carefully add the meatballs and any liquid from their bowl. Add salt to taste. Simmer gently until the sauce is very creamy and aromatic, and the meatballs are heated through.

Transfer to a serving dish. Garnish with a swirl of the thick cream, and a sprinkling of garam masala, chopped herbs and toasted almonds.

SERVES 6–8

Devil's curry

750 g pork leg or shoulder

2 tablespoons soy sauce

2 tablespoons rice vinegar

8 shallots, finely sliced

1 stalk lemongrass, chopped

3–4 fresh hot red chillies, slit and deseeded

4-cm piece fresh galangal, chopped (optional)

2 tablespoons peanut oil

4 cloves garlic, crushed

2-cm piece fresh ginger, finely chopped

1 teaspoon shrimp paste

1½ teaspoons black mustard seeds, crushed

1 teaspoon ground turmeric

salt and black pepper

2 tablespoons crushed candlenuts or macadamia nuts

Cut pork into cubes. Place in a dish, add soy sauce and vinegar, and mix well. Leave for 1 hour, turning occasionally.

In a heavy pan sauté the shallots, lemongrass, chillies and galangal in the oil for about 2 minutes. Add the garlic, ginger, shrimp paste, mustard seeds and turmeric, and cook for 2 minutes over moderate heat, stirring frequently. Stir in the pork, add 1½ cups water, season with salt and pepper, and cover the pan. Cook over moderate heat for 15 minutes without stirring, then remove the lid, stir well and cook for a further 10 minutes.

Stir in the crushed nuts, check seasoning, and continue to cook until the pork is very tender and the liquid well reduced.

SERVES 4–6

A pork curry from Burma

1 kg pork belly

½ cup finely chopped onion

1 head garlic, peeled and finely chopped

2 teaspoons finely chopped fresh ginger

6–8 shallots, finely chopped

2 tablespoons rice vinegar

1 tablespoon sesame oil

2 hot red chillies, deseeded and finely chopped

1 teaspoon ground turmeric

2 tablespoons peanut oil

1 teaspoon shrimp paste

salt and black pepper

thinly sliced fresh red chillies, for garnish

Cut the pork into bite-sized pieces and place in a dish with the onion, garlic, ginger, shallots, vinegar, sesame oil, chillies and turmeric. Mix thoroughly, and leave to marinate for 1–2 hours.

Heat the peanut oil in a nonstick pan and fry the shrimp paste, mashing it as it cooks, then add the pork in batches and cook until well coloured. Add water to not quite cover the meat, season with salt and pepper, and bring to the boil. Reduce heat and simmer uncovered, stirring often, until the pork is very tender and the sauce reduced.

Serve garnished with thinly sliced chillies.

SERVES 6

Thai pork and green beans in red curry

6 green beans, sliced diagonally

400 g pork fillets

2 tablespoons vegetable oil

1 tablespoon Thai Red Curry Paste (page 19)

1 teaspoon palm sugar or soft brown sugar

1 fresh red chilli, deseeded and cut into strips

¼ cup coconut cream

2 kaffir lime leaves, very finely shredded (optional)

2–3 sprigs fresh Thai basil, leaves stripped

fish sauce or salt, to taste

Drop the beans into a small saucepan of rapidly boiling salted water. Cook for 2 minutes, and drain.

Cut the pork into thin slices. Heat oil in a nonstick pan over very high heat and stir-fry the pork for about 30 seconds or until it changes colour, then remove. Add the curry paste and sugar to the pan, and stir-fry for 2 minutes until the paste is very fragrant. Add the chilli and coconut cream and mix well, then return pork and beans to the pan and stir everything together for a minute only.

Stir in the lime and basil leaves before serving and season to taste with fish sauce or salt.

SERVES 4

Pork vindaloo

12 dried red chillies

2 teaspoons ground sweet
paprika

12 black peppercorns

1 teaspoon cumin seeds

1 tablespoon coriander seeds

½ teaspoon fennel seeds

1 tablespoon tamarind water

1 tablespoon white vinegar

750 g pork leg or shoulder,
cut into 2-cm cubes

1 cinnamon stick

12 curry leaves (or use
2–3 bay leaves)

3 star anise

6 cloves

4 tablespoons oil

2 medium-sized onions,
chopped

salt

soft brown sugar

Soak the chillies in hot water for 20 minutes, then drain and place in a food
processor or spice grinder (remove seeds for a milder dish, if preferred).
Add the peppercorns and the cumin, coriander and fennel seeds, and grind
to a paste, then add the tamarind water and vinegar and grind again,
making it very smooth.

Place the pork in a wide flat dish and smear on the marinade, stirring and turning the meat until evenly coated. Scatter with the whole spices and curry or bay leaves, and set aside for at least 1 hour, to absorb the flavours. Stir up every 20 minutes.

Heat the oil in a heavy-based pan and fry the onions until well and evenly coloured (about 6 minutes). Add the marinated pork and cook over high heat, stirring constantly, for about 3 minutes. Add water to barely cover, and salt to taste, and cook until the meat is meltingly tender (about 50 minutes). Check seasonings, adding extra salt and a little sugar, if needed.

SERVES 6

Thai red curry pork

500 g pork leg or fillets

1 medium-sized carrot, sliced

3 tablespoons coconut cream

3–6 teaspoons Thai Red Curry
Paste (page 19)

1 stalk lemongrass, slit
lengthways

1 cup coconut milk

1½ tablespoons fish sauce

1 fresh green chilli, deseeded
and sliced

1 fresh red chilli, deseeded
and sliced

3 kaffir lime leaves

1 tablespoon tamarind water
or fresh lime juice

1 teaspoon sugar

50 g sliced bamboo shoots

salt, if needed

fresh basil leaves

Cut the pork into very thin slices and set aside. Cook the carrot slices in boiling salted water, until just tender.

Heat a wok and cook the coconut cream over high heat until it is oily around the edges. Add the curry paste and lemongrass and heat for 2 minutes until very fragrant. Add the coconut milk, fish sauce, chillies, lime leaves, tamarind water or lime juice, plus the sugar, and bring to the boil. Simmer for 2 minutes.

Reduce heat to low and add the sliced pork, bamboo shoots and carrot. Season with salt if needed. Cook for 2–3 minutes. Stir in basil leaves and serve.

SERVES 4–6

Sri Lankan liver curry

400 g calf liver, sliced

4 dried chillies

2 teaspoons coriander seeds

1½ teaspoons cumin seeds

½ teaspoon fennel seeds

½ teaspoon brown mustard seeds

3–4 tablespoons ghee or oil

2 medium onions, thinly sliced

1 extra medium onion, roughly chopped

3 cloves garlic, chopped

4-cm stalk lemongrass, chopped

8 curry leaves

4–5 tablespoons coconut milk

salt and black pepper

Cut liver into 3-cm pieces. Place in a dish, cover with milk or water and set aside. In a dry pan roast the chillies, coriander, cumin, fennel and mustard seeds until browned. Grind to a fine powder.

Fry the sliced onions in the ghee or oil until brown and crisp. Set aside. Grind the chopped onion to a paste with the garlic and lemongrass. Drain liver and pat dry. Reheat pan and fry curry leaves for a few seconds, then add liver and fry until lightly coloured. Remove to a plate.

Fry the ground spices briefly. Add the onion paste and cook, stirring often, until well cooked and aromatic. Add the coconut milk, salt and pepper, and simmer for 3 minutes, stirring often. Return the liver and fried onions to the pan and simmer gently for a few minutes before serving.

SERVES 4–6

Liver masala

300 g calf liver

1 cup milk

2 tablespoons ghee or oil

1 large onion, finely sliced

3 tomatoes, deseeded and
chopped

3 cloves garlic, crushed

3–4 thin slices fresh ginger

1–2 fresh green chillies,
deseeded and sliced

2 teaspoons Garam Masala
(page 18)

½ teaspoon ground turmeric

3 tablespoons natural yoghurt

salt and black pepper

chopped fresh herbs
(e.g. mint, coriander)

Trim and thinly slice the liver. Soak in the milk for 10 minutes, then drain and pat dry with paper towels.

Heat the ghee in a nonstick pan and fry the onion until well coloured, then add the tomatoes, garlic and ginger and cook over reasonably low heat for about 8 minutes, until soft and pulpy.

Add the liver, chillies, spices and yoghurt with a few tablespoons of cold water, and simmer gently until the liver is tender (5–10 minutes), adding a little extra water if the sauce becomes too thick.

Season to taste with salt and pepper and stir in the herbs before serving.

SERVES 4

Indonesian curried liver

3 tablespoons peanut
   or vegetable oil
400 g lamb or calf liver, sliced
1 small onion, sliced
1 clove garlic, chopped
1-cm piece fresh ginger, grated
4–5 curry leaves (optional)
1 cup coconut milk

1 tablespoon tamarind water
½ teaspoon ground turmeric
1–1½ teaspoons ground chilli
salt and black pepper
1 fresh hot green chilli,
   deseeded and thinly sliced
1 fresh hot red chilli, deseeded
   and thinly sliced

Heat the oil in a frying pan and fry the liver until sealed and lightly browned on both sides. Remove to a plate, and cover.

Sauté the onion, garlic, ginger and curry leaves in the same pan until lightly coloured, add the coconut milk, ¾ cup water, and the tamarind water, turmeric, ground chilli, salt and pepper, and bring to the boil. Simmer briskly for 2 minutes, then lower the heat and return the liver to the pan. Simmer gently for about 12 minutes, until the liver is very tender and the sauce thick. Adjust seasonings, stir in the chilli and serve.

SERVES 4–6

Red kangaroo curry with pineapple

3 cups coconut milk

½–1 tablespoon Thai Red
Curry Paste (page 19)

1 stalk lemongrass, slit
lengthways

500 g kangaroo rump, partially
frozen

3 kaffir lime leaves

1–3 fresh mild red chillies,
slit and deseeded

3 tablespoons coconut cream

3 thick slices fresh pineapple,
cut into chunks

fish sauce and/or salt

fresh Thai basil leaves

Pour the coconut milk into a saucepan and boil gently for about 6 minutes until a layer of oil separates. Add the curry paste and lemongrass and cook another 2–3 minutes.

Cut the kangaroo meat into paper-thin strips 4 cm × 3 cm. Add meat to the curry, together with the lime leaves and chillies, and simmer for 2–3 minutes. Stir in coconut cream and pineapple, and season to taste with fish sauce, and/or salt. Tip into a serving dish and garnish with basil leaves just before serving.

Partly freezing the meat will allow you to cut it into the paper-thin slices needed for this recipe. To remain tender, it must cook in minutes.

SERVES 6

Vegetables and eggs

Hindus, Sikhs and some Buddhists are prohibited from consuming most animal flesh, so it is not surprising that Asia and Southeast Asian countries boast an incredible range of vegetable and other non-meat curry dishes.

Southern Indian vegetarian cuisine is about flamboyantly spiced vegetables in sizzling, palate-teasing sauces. It showcases vegetables simmered, braised, slow-cooked and fried, floating in tingling curry, dripping spicy pastes. Thai cuisine also highlights the fresh natural taste of vegetables, braising root vegetables in thick creamy red curries, bathing greens in emerald and turmeric-gold sauces, challenging palates with fiery flavours.

Curried vegetables and egg dishes are deliciously versatile. Serve them as starters, as side dishes with grilled meats and other curries, or for the main course of a vegetarian meal, with rice, flat bread or a salad.

Creamy pumpkin curry

1½ tablespoons ghee or oil

375 g pumpkin, peeled and diced

½ teaspoon ground cumin

¼ teaspoon ground turmeric

½ cup milk or thin cream

1 fresh green chilli, slit and deseeded

2 bay leaves

salt and black pepper

1⅓ teaspoons black mustard seeds

½ teaspoon cumin seeds

extra tablespoon ghee or oil

Heat the ghee or oil in a medium-sized saucepan and fry the pumpkin with the cumin and turmeric for 1 minute, stirring constantly. Add the milk or cream, chilli, bay leaves, salt and pepper to taste, and cover. Cook over low heat until the pumpkin is tender and the liquid absorbed (about 7 minutes).

In a small pan fry the mustard and cumin seeds in the extra ghee or oil, until they are popping and spluttering. Tip the pumpkin into a serving dish and pour the spiced oil over.

SERVES 4

Spicy braised pumpkin with tamarind

3 cloves garlic, chopped

1 fresh red chilli, split and deseeded

1 medium onion, roughly chopped

3 tablespoons ghee or oil

1 medium onion, very thinly sliced

600 g pumpkin, peeled, seeds removed and flesh diced

2 teaspoons tamarind concentrate

1 cup water

½ teaspoon sugar

salt and black pepper

1½ teaspoons Garam Masala (page 18)

2 tablespoons finely chopped fresh coriander or mint

Grind garlic, chilli and onion to a paste in a food processor or blender.

Heat the ghee or oil in a heavy saucepan or nonstick pan and fry the sliced onion until golden-brown and crisp. Remove with a slotted spoon and set aside. Fry the pumpkin until lightly coloured. Add the onion–garlic paste and cook, stirring often, for about 5 minutes over medium heat. Add the tamarind, water, sugar, salt and pepper, and simmer, uncovered, until the pumpkin is tender and much of the liquid boiled away.

Check seasonings, add garam masala and stir in the herbs and fried onion just before serving.

SERVES 4

Pumpkin with tomato and spices

2 tablespoons ghee or oil

½ teaspoon mustard
 or cumin seeds

500 g pumpkin, peeled and
 cut into 2-cm cubes

1 small onion, thinly sliced

1.5-cm piece fresh ginger, grated

2 cloves garlic, crushed

4 roma tomatoes, deseeded
 and chopped

½ teaspoon ground turmeric

½ teaspoon ground chilli
 or chilli flakes

salt

lemon juice

Heat the ghee or oil in a saucepan with a heavy base and fry the mustard or cumin seeds until they pop and splutter. Add the pumpkin and toss in the pan until coated with the spicy oil.

Cover and cook over medium heat for 5 minutes, then add the onion, ginger and garlic and cook, uncovered, for 1–2 minutes, stirring frequently.

Add the tomatoes, turmeric, chilli and salt to taste, and cover again. Cook over low heat until pumpkin is tender and the tomatoes reduced to a thick sauce (about 6 minutes). Check seasonings and add lemon juice to taste.

SERVES 4–6

Masala cabbage

2 tablespoons oil or ghee

3 cups shredded cabbage

1 onion, thinly sliced

2 teaspoons crushed fresh garlic

½ teaspoon ground chilli

1 teaspoon ground turmeric

1 teaspoon salt

1 teaspoon Garam Masala (page 18)

lemon juice

Heat the oil or ghee in a frying pan and sauté the cabbage, onion and garlic until lightly coloured. Add ground chilli, turmeric and salt, cover and cook over low heat until tender.

Uncover pan, raise the heat to boil off excess liquid, then sprinkle with garam masala and add lemon juice to taste.

SERVES 4–6

Cheese and peas in mild curry

250 g frozen peas

150 g paneer cheese

2–3 tablespoons ghee or oil

1 medium-sized onion,
    finely chopped

1.5-cm piece fresh ginger, grated

3 spring onions, finely chopped

1–2 fresh hot green chillies,
    deseeded and chopped

1 teaspoon salt

1 teaspoon Garam Masala
    (page 18)

½ teaspoon sugar

chopped fresh coriander
    or mint

Boil the peas in lightly salted water until almost cooked (about 4 minutes).
Drain, reserving ½ cup of the water.

Cut the paneer into small cubes and fry in the ghee or oil until golden.
Remove with a slotted spoon and set aside.

Fry the onion in the same oil until soft and lightly coloured (about 4 minutes),
then increase heat to medium-high. Add the ginger, spring onions, chillies,
salt, garam masala and sugar, and cook for 1 minute, stirring constantly.
Return the peas and paneer to the pan and add the reserved cooking
water. Simmer gently until the flavours are absorbed (about 3 minutes).

SERVES 4

Saag paneer

500 g chopped fresh or
   frozen spinach

300 g paneer cheese

3 tablespoons ghee or oil

1–2 cloves garlic, crushed with
   1 teaspoon salt

2 teaspoons Garam Masala
   (page 18)

½ teaspoon grated or
   ground nutmeg

⅓ cup pouring cream
   or natural yoghurt

white pepper

Place fresh spinach in a saucepan with ½ cup water and cook, tightly covered, for 4–5 minutes. Tip into a colander to drain. (If using frozen spinach, thaw in a colander.)

Cut the cheese into 2-cm cubes. Heat the ghee or oil in a frying pan and fry the cheese until golden on the surface (about 1 minute), stirring and turning constantly. Add the garlic, garam masala and nutmeg and fry briefly, then pour in the cream or yoghurt and bring to a simmer. Stir in the drained spinach, with pepper to taste and extra salt if needed, and simmer gently until the spices infuse the cheese and spinach (about 3 minutes).

❧ Paneer is a fresh, unsalted, cottage-style Indian cheese. It is available in Asian and health-food stores and some supermarkets.

SERVES 4

Spinach bhartha

600 g fresh spinach (or use 500 g
  frozen spinach)
2 tablespoons ghee or butter
2 cloves garlic, crushed with
  1 teaspoon salt
1.5-cm piece fresh ginger, grated
1 teaspoon ground mild red chilli
½ teaspoon grated nutmeg
2–3 tablespoons thick cream
  or sour cream

Trim stalks from fresh spinach, if using, and rinse the leaves well. Shake out water, but do not dry. Place fresh or frozen spinach in a saucepan and cover tightly. Cook over medium heat for about 4 minutes, until wilted (frozen spinach may take a few minutes longer), then tip into a colander to drain.

In the same saucepan heat the ghee or butter and sauté the garlic and ginger over medium heat. Add the chilli and nutmeg, return the spinach and cook, stirring, for about 1 minute. Add the cream or sour cream and simmer gently for 2 minutes. Check and adjust seasoning before serving.

SERVES 4

Coconut-simmered vegetables

1 medium-sized eggplant,
  cut into 1-cm cubes

1 cup cauliflower florets

1 cup sliced snake or green beans

1 carrot, peeled and sliced

1 onion, sliced

salt

1 teaspoon ground cumin

1 teaspoon ground turmeric

1 cup grated fresh coconut

½ punnet cherry tomatoes,
  halved

¾ cup fresh bean sprouts

1 teaspoon black mustard seeds

1–2 fresh green chillies,
  deseeded and sliced

6–8 curry leaves (optional)

2 tablespoons oil or ghee

Place the eggplant, cauliflower, beans, carrot and onion in a saucepan and season with salt, cumin and turmeric. Add ½–1 cup water, cover the pan tightly, and cook over medium heat for about 5 minutes. Add the coconut, tomatoes and bean sprouts to the pan and cook for a further 3–4 minutes, until vegetables are tender.

In a small pan fry the mustard seeds, chillies and curry leaves in the oil or ghee. Transfer vegetables to a serving dish and splash the spiced oil over just before serving.

SERVES 6

Vegetable curry

1 medium-sized onion, chopped

3 tablespoons ghee or oil

2–3 cloves garlic, crushed

4-cm piece fresh ginger, sliced

3 medium-sized potatoes, peeled and cut into 1.5-cm cubes

1 small turnip, peeled and cut into 1.5-cm cubes

2 medium-sized carrots, peeled and cut into 1.5-cm cubes

1 teaspoon ground turmeric

2 teaspoons ground hot chilli

3 teaspoons Garam Masala (page 18)

1 medium eggplant, cut into 2-cm cubes

½ medium-sized cauliflower, separated into small florets

4–5 small tomatoes, quartered

100 g green beans or okra, sliced diagonally

In a large saucepan fry the onion in the ghee or oil until lightly coloured. Add the garlic and ginger and fry briefly, then add the potatoes, turnip, carrots, turmeric and chilli, and half the garam masala. Add water to barely cover and bring to the boil, adding salt to taste. Cook on high heat for about 8 minutes, stirring frequently.

Reduce heat to medium. Add remaining vegetable to pan and continue to cook, tightly covered, until vegetables are tender and liquid reduced. Adjust seasoning before serving sprinkled with the remaining garam masala.

SERVES 8

Curried green beans

500 g green beans, sliced diagonally

1 tablespoon mild curry powder or paste

6 shallots, finely sliced

1 hot green chilli, deseeded
   and finely chopped

4–6 curry leaves (optional)

⅓ teaspoon ground turmeric

½ cup coconut cream

⅓ cup water or vegetable stock

salt

fresh lemon juice

Place all the ingredients, except the lemon juice, in a medium-sized saucepan and simmer over low-medium heat for 10–15 minutes until beans are tender and the sauce quite thick.

Check seasonings, adjusting salt as needed, and add a squeeze of lemon juice just before serving.

SERVES 6–8 AS A SIDE DISH

Mushrooms, peas and tomatoes in a creamy curry sauce

250 g button mushrooms

1 punnet cherry tomatoes

4 tablespoons ghee, oil or butter

1 teaspoon Garam Masala (page 18)

½ teaspoon ground white pepper

1¼ teaspoons salt

¼ teaspoon ground turmeric

200 g frozen peas

1 cup cream

1 tablespoon chopped fresh coriander or mint leaves

finely chopped fresh green chilli (optional)

Wipe the mushrooms with paper towel, if necessary. Cut the cherry tomatoes in half.

Heat the ghee, oil or butter and sauté the mushrooms for about 2 minutes. Add the garam masala, pepper, salt and turmeric, stirring for a few seconds over high heat.

Add the halved tomatoes and the peas, and stir over high heat for 30 seconds, then add the cream, cover and reduce heat. Simmer for about 6 minutes, until ingredients are tender and aromatic.

Before serving, stir in the coriander or mint, check and adjust seasonings, and add chilli if you want.

SERVES 4 – 6

Roasted masala potatoes

500 g small potatoes

salt

⅓ teaspoon asafoetida powder

4 cloves

1½ teaspoons cumin seeds

2 teaspoons ground coriander

1 fresh green chilli, deseeded and chopped

1 teaspoon grated fresh ginger

2 tablespoons ghee or oil

Garam Masala (page 18), dried mint and ground chilli, to serve

Preheat oven to 180°.

Cook the potatoes (peeled or unpeeled, as preferred) in well salted boiling water for 10 minutes, until nearly tender. Drain well, then put lid on saucepan and shake vigorously to ruffle the surface of the potatoes – this helps them to become crisper and crunchier when roasted.

In an ovenproof dish fry the asafoetida, cloves, cumin seeds, coriander, chilli and ginger in the ghee or oil until very fragrant. Transfer the potatoes to the dish, turning to coat with the oil and spices.

Roast in preheated oven for about 30 minutes. Sprinkle with garam masala, dried mint and ground chilli before serving.

SERVES 4–6

Potato and onion curry

3 tablespoons vegetable oil

½ teaspoon black mustard seeds

2 large potatoes, peeled and
  cut into 2-cm cubes

1 large onion, cut into
  2-cm cubes

3 cloves garlic, sliced

1 fresh red chilli, deseeded
  and sliced

1 fresh green chilli, deseeded
  and sliced

2-cm piece fresh ginger,
  shredded

¾ teaspoon ground turmeric

2 teaspoons ground coriander

½ teaspoon asafoetida powder

1 tablespoon toasted, shredded
  coconut, for garnish

Heat the oil in a medium-sized saucepan and add the mustard seeds.
Cover and cook over high heat until the seeds begin to pop and splutter,
then add the potatoes and toss them around in the pan until evenly coated
with the oil and spices. Cover, and cook over medium heat for about
4 minutes, shaking the pan occasionally.

Add the onion, garlic, chillies, ginger and turmeric and cook, again shaking
the pan occasionally, for about 6 minutes. Last of all, add the coriander
and asafoetida, and continue to cook, tightly covered, until the vegetables
are tender (1–3 minutes). Tip into a serving dish and sprinkle with the
toasted coconut.

SERVES 4

Alu mattar
(braised potato and peas)

2 tablespoons vegetable or
    peanut oil

½ teaspoon cumin seeds

2 large potatoes, peeled and cut
    into 2-cm cubes

1 fresh hot green chilli, slit
    and deseeded

1-cm piece fresh ginger,
    shredded

2 cloves garlic, finely chopped

2 teaspoons ground coriander

1 teaspoon ground cumin

1 cup canned crushed tomatoes

salt and black pepper

½–¾ teaspoon ground turmeric

1 cup frozen peas

1 teaspoon sugar

In a medium-sized saucepan heat the oil and fry the cumin seeds until they pop and splutter. Add the potatoes, chilli, ginger and garlic, and toss in the oil to seal, then add ½ cup water, plus the coriander, cumin, tomatoes, salt, pepper and turmeric.

Cover the saucepan and bring to the boil. Reduce heat and simmer for 2 minutes, then uncover the pan and allow everything to bubble gently until the potato is almost cooked and the sauce well reduced. Add the peas and sugar and cook for a few minutes until soft. Check seasonings and serve.

SERVES 4–6

Cauliflower, pea and potato curry

⅓ cup vegetable oil

½ teaspoon cumin seeds

350 g cauliflower, separated into large florets

180 g potato, peeled and diced

1 cup frozen peas

1 fresh hot green chilli, deseeded and chopped

2 cloves garlic, chopped

1-cm piece fresh ginger, chopped

½ teaspoon ground turmeric

1½ teaspoons ground cumin

1½ teaspoons ground coriander

½ teaspoon ground hot chilli or chilli flakes

1 teaspoon salt

1 teaspoon sugar

Heat the oil in a saucepan, add the cumin seeds and fry, covered, until they pop and splutter. Add the cauliflower and potato, and shake the pan to coat them with the oil and spices. Add ½ cup water, cover the pan again and cook for about 7 minutes, until vegetables are almost tender.

Stir in the peas and add the chilli, garlic, ginger, ground spices, salt and sugar. Cover again and cook over medium heat, stirring occasionally, until tender (about 5 minutes).

Check seasonings before serving.

SERVES 4–6

Masaman curry of potatoes and green beans

700 g potatoes, peeled and
cut into 2-cm cubes

2 cups coconut milk

1 teaspoon salt

1½–2 tablespoons masaman
curry paste

1 cinnamon stick

2 bay leaves

4 cloves

150 g green or snake beans,
diagonally sliced

4 spring onions, sliced

2 tablespoons fish sauce

2 tablespoons crunchy peanut
butter (optional)

1 tablespoon tamarind water

1 teaspoon soft brown sugar

extra salt, plus black pepper

Place the potatoes in a saucepan with the coconut milk, salt, curry paste, cinnamon, bay leaves and cloves. Bring to the boil, then reduce heat and simmer, covered, until almost tender (about 8 minutes).

Add the remaining ingredients and simmer gently for a few more minutes, uncovered, until the beans and potato are quite tender and the curry sauce very fragrant and slightly thickened.

Season to taste with salt and pepper before serving.

SERVES 4–6

Malaysian eggplant

1 cup vegetable or peanut oil

3–4 slender Asian eggplants, cut into 4-cm chunks

6 spring onions, chopped

6 cloves garlic, finely chopped

1 teaspoon grated fresh galangal or ginger

2 fresh hot green chillies, deseeded and sliced

1½ teaspoons ground cumin

3 cardamom pods, cracked

1 cinnamon stick

1 teaspoon fennel seeds, crushed

2 tablespoons mild Malaysian curry paste

1 cup coconut cream

salt and black pepper

Heat the oil to very hot. Fry the eggplant pieces for about 5 minutes, turning frequently. Remove with a slotted spoon and set aside to drain.

Pour off all but 2 tablespoons of the oil in the pan and fry the onions for 4 minutes over medium heat, stirring. Add garlic, galangal or ginger, and chillies, fry for 1 minute, then stir in the spices and curry paste and increase the heat. Cook, stirring, for 1 minute.

Add the coconut cream and fried eggplant to the pan, bring to the boil, then reduce heat and simmer until eggplant is tender (about 10 minutes). Season to taste with salt and pepper before serving.

SERVES 4

West Coast eggplant curry

2 teaspoons coriander seeds

½ teaspoon cumin seeds

¾ cup desiccated coconut

500 g small, oval-shaped
eggplants

¼ cup vegetable oil

½ teaspoon black mustard seeds

2–4 fresh hot red chillies, slit
and deseeded

2 large cloves garlic, chopped

2-cm piece fresh ginger, grated

4–6 curry leaves (preferably
fresh)

2 large onions, finely chopped

⅓ teaspoon ground turmeric

2 teaspoons tamarind
concentrate

In a small pan dry-fry the coriander and cumin seeds and the desiccated coconut until the coconut is golden-brown and the spices very aromatic. Grind to a powder, and add enough water to make a smooth paste.

With a sharp knife make several deep incisions across each eggplant, at 1.5-cm intervals (this helps them cook through). Heat a pan large enough to fit the eggplant in one layer. In it heat the oil to medium and fry the mustard seeds and chillies for 1 minute. Add the garlic, ginger, curry leaves, onions and turmeric, and fry briefly. Lower the heat and cook, stirring frequently, until the onions are softened and well browned (about 10 minutes). >

Add the prepared spice paste to the pan with a few tablespoons of cold water and cook for a further 5 minutes. Nestle the eggplants amongst the onions, scooping some of the spicy sauce over them. Mix the tamarind concentrate with 1 cup water and pour into the pan.

Cover tightly and cook gently until eggplants are tender (about 20 minutes). Check from time to time, stirring carefully to prevent onions sticking, adding a little extra water if needed.

SERVES 6

Eggplant and tomato curry

1 cup vegetable or peanut oil

500 g slender Asian eggplants, cut into 3-cm pieces

1 teaspoon cumin seeds

1.5-cm piece fresh ginger, chopped

3 cloves garlic, chopped

2 cups canned crushed tomatoes, or chopped fresh tomatoes

1 fresh hot red chilli, slit and deseeded

1/3 teaspoon ground turmeric

2 teaspoons ground coriander

3/4 teaspoon sugar

salt

chopped fresh mint or coriander leaves

Heat the oil in a frying pan or wok and fry the eggplant in batches over high heat, until browned. Set aside in a colander to drain.

Pour off all but 1 tablespoon of the oil in the pan and add the cumin seeds, frying until they pop and splutter. Add the ginger and garlic and fry briefly, then pour in the tomatoes and add the chilli, turmeric, coriander, sugar and a large pinch of salt. Bring to the boil, reduce heat and simmer for 5 minutes, then add ½ cup cold water and simmer a further 5–6 minutes, until the sauce is very fragrant. >

Add the eggplant and reduce heat to low. Simmer for 15–20 minutes, stirring occasionally. Check and adjust seasonings and stir in the fresh herbs before transferring to a serving dish.

SERVES 6

Okra in curry spices

24–28 small okra (or 12–18 larger ones), thickly sliced

3 tablespoons vegetable oil or ghee

1 teaspoon cumin seeds

½ teaspoon fennel seeds

2 cloves garlic, finely chopped

1-cm piece fresh ginger, finely chopped

1 small onion, finely chopped

1 medium-sized very ripe tomato, deseeded and chopped

¾ teaspoon salt

fresh lemon juice

Rinse okra in cold water and drain well.

Heat the oil or ghee in a large pan and fry the cumin and fennel seeds over medium heat until they begin to pop and splutter. Add the garlic, ginger and onion, and fry for 1–2 minutes, stirring. Add the chopped tomato, okra and salt and cook, tightly covered, for about 8 minutes until tender, stirring occasionally. Squeeze lemon juice over just before serving.

SERVES 4 AS A SIDE DISH

Whole masala cauliflower

CAULIFLOWER

1 medium-sized cauliflower

3-cm piece fresh ginger, grated

4 cloves garlic, crushed

1–2 fresh hot green chillies,
deseeded and finely chopped

1 teaspoon salt

½ teaspoon Garam Masala
(page 18)

2 teaspoons vinegar or fresh
lemon juice

grated cheese (optional)

MASALA SAUCE

2 tablespoons coriander seeds

4 tablespoons desiccated coconut

1 teaspoon cumin seeds

3 tablespoons ghee or oil

1 large onion, very finely chopped

3 cloves garlic, finely chopped

pinch of ground cloves

½ teaspoon ground nutmeg
or mace

2 teaspoons Garam Masala
(page 18)

¾ cup natural yoghurt

chopped fresh herbs
(e.g. mint, coriander)

Preheat oven or grill to 190°C.

Wash the cauliflower and set upside down to drain. Trim the stem flat and
select a saucepan which will hold the cauliflower upright while it cooks. >

Grind the ginger, garlic, chillies, salt, garam masala and vinegar or lemon juice to a paste. Spoon paste into the cauliflower, between the florets.

Place cauliflower in the saucepan, stem downwards, and add about 4 cm of water. Cover and steam for about 15 minutes, until the cauliflower is tender. Transfer to a well-greased ovenproof dish.

While the cauliflower is cooking, prepare the masala sauce. First toast the coriander, coconut and cumin in a dry pan until well browned and very fragrant, then grind to a fine powder. Heat the ghee or oil in a saucepan and fry the onion for 6–8 minutes over medium heat, until very soft and lightly coloured. Add the garlic and fry briefly, then add all the spices and yoghurt and cook, stirring, until well blended (about 2 minutes).

Spoon sauce over the cauliflower, covering evenly. If you like, spread a little grated cheese on top. Place cauliflower in preheated oven or grill and heat until the top is brown. Garnish with the chopped herbs.

SERVES 4–6

Vegetable koftas in curry sauce

600 g potatoes

2 tablespoons finely chopped
fresh coriander or mint

1 teaspoon ground chilli

1 teaspoon salt

1½ teaspoons Garam Masala
(page 18)

1 egg, beaten

chickpea flour (besan)

oil or ghee for deep-frying

CURRY SAUCE

1 large onion, finely chopped

2 tablespoons ghee or oil

4 cloves garlic, finely chopped

2-cm piece fresh ginger, grated

2 tablespoons desiccated coconut

2–4 teaspoons mild Indian curry
paste (korma paste)

1 cup natural yoghurt

salt to taste

chopped fresh green chilli and
coriander

Boil or bake the potatoes in their skins and when completely tender remove
from the heat. Leave to cool, then peel. Place potato in a bowl and mash
until smooth. Mix in the chopped coriander or mint, the chilli, salt and
garam masala, and form mixture into oval shapes about 6 cm long. Dip into
beaten egg, then coat thickly with chickpea flour. If time allows, refrigerate
koftas for 2–3 hours so they firm up before frying. >

Heat 3 cm of oil or ghee in a nonstick pan. Fry the koftas 5 or 6 at a time until golden-brown, turning once or twice. Carefully transfer to a serving dish and keep warm.

To make the curry sauce, sauté the onion in the ghee or oil until well browned. Add the garlic, ginger, coconut and curry paste, and sauté for 2–3 minutes on medium heat, stirring constantly. Pour in the yoghurt and 1 cup water, then bring barely to the boil, reduce heat and simmer for about 8 minutes or until the sauce is very thick and fragrant. Season with salt.

To serve, pour sauce over the koftas and scatter with chopped chilli and coriander.

SERVES 4–6

Cashew-nut curry

2½ cups thin coconut milk

1 cup raw cashew nuts

1 medium-sized onion, finely sliced

3 fresh green chillies, split and deseeded

½ pandanus leaf, bruised (optional)

6–10 curry leaves

½ teaspoon ground turmeric

1 cinnamon stick

1 teaspoon crushed fresh garlic

1 teaspoon crushed fresh ginger

salt and black pepper

2 teaspoons roasted Sri Lankan spices (page 98)

Pour coconut milk into a saucepan and add everything except the roasted spices. Bring almost to the boil, then reduce heat and simmer for 30 minutes.

Add the roasted spices to the pan and continue to simmer, stirring occasionally, until cashews are tender and the sauce thickened. Check seasonings, and discard pandanus leaf (if used) before serving.

SERVES 4–6

Add the bean sprouts, bamboo shoots and chillies to the pan and simmer for a minute or two. Check seasonings, adding salt and pepper to taste and a generous squeeze of lemon or lime juice. Garnish with the herbs before serving.

SERVES 4

Coconut-coated vegetables

500 g water spinach or other
    Asian greens

1–2 fresh hot green chillies,
    deseeded and shredded

2 tablespoons oil

½ teaspoon ground turmeric

8 curry leaves

1 medium-sized onion,
    very thinly sliced

½ cup grated fresh or
    desiccated coconut

salt and black pepper

lemon juice

Wash, trim and shred the greens. Place in a covered saucepan and steam for 3 minutes.

In a frying pan sauté the chillies briefly in the oil, then add the turmeric, curry leaves and onion and fry for 3–4 minutes until the onion is lightly browned. Add the coconut and the steamed vegetables and toss together until well mixed.

Season to taste with salt, pepper and lemon juice before serving.

SERVES 4

Spiced chickpeas

500 g canned chickpeas

2½ tablespoons ghee or oil

3-cm piece fresh ginger, grated

1 large onion, very finely chopped

3 teaspoons Garam Masala (page 18)

1–2 fresh hot green chillies, deseeded and chopped

2 large ripe tomatoes, deseeded and chopped

salt and black pepper

2–3 tablespoons chopped fresh coriander or mint

1–2 tablespoons freshly squeezed lemon juice

Drain the chickpeas, reserving the liquid.

Heat the ghee or oil in a medium-sized saucepan and fry the ginger and onion over medium heat for about 5 minutes, until lightly coloured and fragrant. Stir in the garam masala and stir for 30–40 seconds, then add the chillies and tomatoes and bring to a simmer. Reduce heat and cook for about 5 minutes, stirring frequently, until thoroughly softened.

Add the chickpeas and enough of their reserved liquid to just cover. Season with salt and pepper and simmer for about 20 minutes, stirring frequently. Add chopped herbs, check seasonings, season to taste with lemon juice and simmer again for 1–2 minutes before serving.

SERVES 4

Bring to the boil, reduce heat and simmer until shallots are cooked and the lentils so tender they are breaking up (this thickens the sauce).

In another pan fry the mustard seeds, curry leaves and chilli (if using) in the remaining oil until very fragrant, then stir into the lentils.

Adjust seasonings, adding salt if needed, a pinch of sugar, and garnish with the chopped herbs.

A sambar is a thin curry, usually fiercely hot, from the south of India where much of the population follows a strict vegetarian diet. It may be served at breakfast or lunch, or enjoyed as a between-meals snack. Dosa, a large, pancake-like flat bread made from a fermented batter, is the traditional accompaniment to a sambar.

SERVES 4 AS A SNACK

Strain the beans and tip into the sauce, simmering for at least 6 minutes over gentle heat.

In a small pan heat the remaining oil and fry the mustard seeds and curry leaves until they pop and rustle.

Pour the beans into a serving dish and swirl the fragrant oil and spices over the top.

SERVES 4–6

Curried red lentils

2 cups dried red lentils

1 teaspoon turmeric

1 teaspoon ground chilli

2 teaspoons ground coriander

1 teaspoon Garam Masala
  (page 18)

1 tablespoon fresh lemon juice

salt

1 medium-sized onion,
  finely sliced

2 tablespoons ghee or oil

1 teaspoon cumin seeds

fresh coriander leaves
  for garnish

Rinse and drain the lentils and place in a saucepan with 3½ cups water, the turmeric, chilli and ground coriander. Bring to the boil, reduce heat and simmer until tender (about 30 minutes). Add the garam masala and lemon juice, with salt to taste.

In a small pan cook the onion in the ghee or oil until almost crisp (about 5 minutes). Add the cumin seeds and continue cooking until the seeds pop and the onion is crisp. Pour onion mixture over the lentils, and serve garnished with the fresh coriander.

SERVES 6

Spiced brown lentils

1½ cups dried brown lentils

1 fresh hot green chilli,
    deseeded and sliced

1 teaspoon ground turmeric

1 medium-sized onion,
    finely sliced

2 cloves garlic, finely chopped

1-cm piece fresh ginger,
    finely chopped

2½ tablespoons vegetable
    or peanut oil

2 ripe tomatoes, deseeded
    and chopped

salt and black pepper

2 teaspoons Garam Masala
    (page 18)

½ teaspoon black mustard seeds

½ teaspoon cumin seeds

chopped fresh coriander
    for garnish

Rinse lentils in cold water, drain well and transfer to a saucepan. Add 3 cups cold water and the chilli and turmeric. Bring to the boil, reduce heat and simmer for about 20 minutes, until lentils are tender but not mushy. Drain.

In a frying pan brown the onion, garlic and ginger in 2 tablespoons of the oil, then add the tomatoes and cook for 2–3 minutes, stirring frequently, until pulpy.

Stir tomato mixture into the lentils, add salt and pepper to taste, and cook for a minute or two, stirring often. Tip into a serving dish. >

Rinse and dry the frying pan and add the remaining oil. When very hot, put in the mustard and cumin seeds to fry until they begin to pop and are very fragrant (about 1 minute).

Pour the oil and spices over the lentils, scatter chopped coriander on top, and serve.

SERVES 4

Curried eggs and vegetables

3 tablespoons ghee or oil

1 medium-sized onion, very
finely chopped

1-cm piece fresh ginger, grated

4 garlic cloves, crushed

1–3 fresh green chillies,
deseeded and finely chopped

1 large potato, peeled and diced

3 roma tomatoes, deseeded
and diced

400 ml coconut milk

1½ teaspoons salt

125 g frozen peas

2 teaspoons Garam Masala
(page 18)

¾ teaspoon ground turmeric

6 hardboiled eggs, shelled

fresh lemon or lime juice,
to taste

handful of chopped fresh
coriander or mint

Heat the ghee or oil in a heavy saucepan and fry the onion, ginger, garlic
and chillies until soft and aromatic (about 5 minutes), stirring frequently.

Add the potato, tomatoes, coconut milk and salt, and enough water to
barely cover. Bring to the boil and simmer for 10 minutes, then add the
peas, garam masala and turmeric and cook for a further 5 minutes.

Cut eggs into wedges and place in a serving dish. Taste curry sauce,
adjusting seasonings and adding a squeeze of lemon or lime juice, and
the chopped herbs. Pour over the eggs, and serve.

SERVES 6

Special ingredients

AJWAIN (also known as carom) is a small, tear-shaped seed with a fragrance similar to thyme. It is sprinkled over tandoori and rice dishes, used in pickles and chutneys, and occasionally in curries. Caraway or celery seeds may be used instead.

ASAFOETIDA is a strong-smelling dried gum used as a seasoning and anti-flatulent, particularly in Indian vegetarian cooking. It has a resinous, garlicky flavour. Available as lumps or granules, and in ground form, it should be used sparingly.

BAMBOO SHOOTS add a distinctive, earthy flavour to Thai curries. If you don't care for them, leave them out. Canned, sliced bamboo shoots are fine, and should be added in the last few minutes of cooking. Any unused shoots should be stored in a container in the refrigerator and will keep fresh for 1 week (change the water daily). Do not freeze.

BEAN SPROUTS should be absolutely fresh and crisp, or they will impart a peculiar, bitter flavour to a curry. Buy only what is required for a recipe. Blanch in boiling water and refresh in cold water before use and then, if you can be bothered, pick off roots and seed pods to give you elegant, delicately flavoured 'silver' sprouts. Bean sprouts will keep freshest on layers of paper towel in a plastic container, in the vegetable crisper; store for up to 4 days.

CANDLENUTS (sometimes known as *buah keras*) are kemiri nuts, a starchy variety grown in Indonesia and used, ground to a paste, to thicken and enrich curries. Candlenuts should not be eaten raw. Raw macadamias or cashews are the best substitute.

CARDAMOM is a delicately flavoured spice comprising small glossy seeds within a smooth pale-green pod. Cardamom pods should be cracked or crushed before use. Ground cardamom can be used instead, at a pinch; as with all ground spices, keep it tightly capped.

CASSIA BARK is similar to cinnamon, though it has a coarser texture and less refined aroma and flavour. It is sold as flat red-brown chips which are used whole, or can be ground to a powder. Cinnamon can be used instead.

COCONUT products bring a smooth creaminess to curry sauces. The white flesh of ripe coconuts is grated and squeezed to extract **COCONUT CREAM**, which in turn is infused in water to produce the thinner product labelled as **COCONUT MILK**. Canned coconut milk and cream is ready to use; **CREAMED COCONUT**, a concentrated form sold in blocks, is grated or chopped and mixed with water before us; **COCONUT MILK POWDER** is mixed into warm water. You can use unsweetened **DESICCATED COCONUT** to produce coconut milk or cream if there's none in the cupboard: to make 2 cups coconut milk, blend or process 1½ cups desiccated coconut with 3 cups hot water (or 1 cup hot milk and 2 cups hot water) until smooth and creamy. Unused coconut products can be frozen in small plastic containers.

EGGPLANTS (ASIAN) come in many forms. Thai **PEA EGGPLANTS** are a tiny, pea-sized green variety, which you can occasionally find fresh in Asian food stores (they can be frozen). Their texture is firm and grainy and they are added whole to curries, sometimes in bunches. There are also white, green and purple eggplants the size of a golfball, which are usually sliced or quartered as a garnish, or added whole to curries. Other varieties include long, slender, white and purple eggplants. The more familiar large globe eggplant is often used as well, usually being cut into chunks and fried in oil before adding to a curry.

FISH SAUCE is to Thai and Vietnamese cooking what soy sauce is to Chinese food. It adds salty flavour to curries, sauces and dressings, but its other attribute, despite its unpleasantly pungent smell, is that it accentuates the flavours of other ingredients. Keep the bottle tightly closed when not in use.

GALANGAL (in Thailand known as *kha*) resembles fresh root ginger but its skin is a deeper tan colour and it bears small, tender pink shoots which are edible and make an attractive garnish. Fresh galangal is available in Asian food stores: it is usually peeled and cut into chunks or slices for use. Fresh ginger can be used instead, but as its flavour is stronger use half the quantity specified. Dried and ground galangal are also available and can be used instead in curry sauces and pastes.

GARAM MASALA is an aromatic blend of spices used to season curries and to sprinkle over finished dishes. Its chief spices are coriander, cumin, peppercorns, cloves, cardamoms, cinnamon and nutmeg, though it can contain many others, following recipes that have been handed down through families over generations. For a recipe to make your own garam masala, see page 18.

GHEE is clarified butter, which keeps for months in the refrigerator, or for weeks in a cool part of the kitchen. It is available in supermarkets as well as Asian food stores. Cooking oil and butter may be substituted.

GINGER should be fresh: choose roots with unwrinkled beige skin, and test for freshness by snapping off one of the nodules. The flesh should be moist, fragrant and a light yellow colour. Keep refrigerated to prevent dehydration: peel and then use in chunks, sliced, shredded, grated or crushed, as required. Crystallised and pink sushi ginger may replace fresh in an emergency, but ground ginger is rarely used in curry cooking.

KAFFIR LIME is a different fruit to the more familiar Tahitian lime, but is becoming more available. Most of its unique, intense fragrance is concentrated in the deep-green, knobbly skin, which can be peeled or grated for use. **KAFFIR LIME LEAVES** have a similar intense fragrance and are added whole, or very finely shredded, to curries. The fresh leaves keep for several weeks; soak dried leaves in hot water before use.

KECAP MANIS is a thick soy sauce sweetened with caramelised sugar. It adds a glossy dark colour and rich sweet–salty flavour as a seasoning or a garnish. It is available in supermarkets as well as Asian food stores.

KOKUM (also known as cocum) is a sour fruit which is sold dried as a seasoning, particularly for fish dishes. It is most commonly found in Indian food stores. You can use lemon juice or tamarind instead.

LEMONGRASS has a tapering, pale-green layered stem with long, willowy leaves; it is the compacted lower section that gives its distinctive citrus flavour. Before use, trim off top and bottom of the stem and discard outer layers if they are dry and coarse; slitting or bruising the stem helps release its wonderful flavour. Buy it fresh in Asian stores and supermarkets (the stems keep for 1–3 weeks in the vegetable crisper), or grow some at home (it likes moisture and heat). Avoid dried lemongrass if possible, but if this is all you can find reconstitute it in hot water before use. Bottled chopped lemongrass, treated with mild citric-acid marinade, is an acceptable substitute and keeps for months in the refrigerator.

PALM SUGAR (labelled variously as *gula melaka*, jaggery, *nam tan peep* or *gula jawa*, depending on the country of origin) is derived from sugar, sago and even coconut palms. Like cane sugar it varies from pale to dark; the darker the colour, the stronger the flavour. It comes in jars, blocks and logs, and is crushed, grated or chopped for use in sauces, dressings and marinades. You can use raw sugar or soft brown sugar instead.

PANDANUS LEAVES (also sold as *daun pandan*, *rampe*, *kewra* or *toey*) give a distinct sweet–smoky fragrance and pale-green colour to many Asian dishes, especially sweets and rice but also to curries. The leaves are available fresh, dried or frozen in Asian food stores. A bottled essence is also available, but should be used with restraint as it is extremely concentrated.

PANEER is a cottage-style, rennet-free pressed cheese that is popular in Indian cookery. It is available in supermarkets as well as Asian food stores, and freezes well.

SAFFRON is an expensive spice, but a little goes a long way. A small pinch of red saffron threads (stigma) or powder is enough to add brilliant yellow colour, a unique and delicate fragrance, and distinctive flavour to curry and rice dishes. Beware imitation saffron powder, which uses artificial dyes and has no flavour.

SAMBAL ULEK (or oelek) is a potent blend of crushed red chillies and salt. Sold in jars, it should be refrigerated after opening, then will last for many months.

SAMBAR MASALA is a hot, tart spice mixture containing ground lentils, pepper and spices. It is used in southern Indian vegetarian cooking, and can be purchased in Indian food stores.

SHRIMP PASTE, a foul-smelling ingredient made from fermented, ground shrimps, is one of the most interesting and little-understood flavourings in curry cooking. Like fish sauce, shrimp paste enlivens other flavours while adding its own complex and salty taste. It goes by various names, including *blacan* (Malay) and *trasi* or *terasi* (Indonesian). *Kapi* (Thai) and *nam rouc* (Vietnamese) are softer, smoother pastes with a more refined flavour. Shrimp paste should be fried in a few teaspoons of oil before using, to release its true flavour. Store in a tightly closed glass (not plastic) jar. No gain without pain – have the exhaust fan on High before you begin!

STAR ANISE is an elegant star-shaped whole spice with an intense anise flavour and aroma. In curries, it can be replaced by fennel or caraway seeds.

TAMARIND is used in curries the way lemon juice is used in the west, to add a tart–sour flavour and to tenderise meat. Tamarind is sold in different forms: the simplest to use is tamarind concentrate or purée, which can be added directly to curries, though I have mostly specified **TAMARIND WATER**. As a general rule, dilute 1 teaspoon of the concentrate in 1 tablespoon of water to make 1 tablespoon tamarind water. Tamarind pulp is also available, but is less convenient to use, as it must be soaked in hot water, mashed and the seeds and pith strained off. Lemon juice can be used as a substitute.

TURMERIC, a relative of ginger, is a root with intensely red-yellow flesh and is used primarily for colouring but also for its distinct earthy flavour. Fresh turmeric can occasionally be found in Asian fresh food stores. Ground turmeric is an acceptable substitute.

VIETNAMESE MINT (also known as Cambodian mint or *rau ram*) has pointed, brown-marked leaves with a pungent, peppery flavour. It is available fresh in Asian food stores and some supermarkets.

WATER SPINACH (sometimes sold as *kangkong*) is a spinach-like vegetable popular in Asian cooking. It is becoming more readily available, but you can use fresh spinach or watercress instead.

Index

PENGUIN BOOKS

Published by the Penguin Group
Penguin Group (Australia)
250 Camberwell Road, Camberwell, Victoria 3124, Australia

New York   Toronto   London   Dublin
New Delhi   Auckland   Johannesburg

Penguin Books Ltd, Registered Offices: 80 Strand, London, WC2R 0RL, England

First published by Penguin Group (Australia), 2007

10 9 8 7 6 5 4 3 2

Text and photographs copyright © Penguin Group (Australia), 2007

Design by Elizabeth Theodosiadis and Claire Tice © Penguin Group (Australia)
Photography by Julie Renouf
Food styling by Linda Brushfield
Scanning and separations by Splitting Image P/L, Clayton, Victoria

Typeset by Post Pre-press Group, Brisbane, Queensland
Printed in China by Everbest Printing Co. Ltd

Many thanks to Freedom Furniture in South Yarra, Provisions in Camberwell, Tempted in Kensington and The Eastern Ingredient in Northcote for their lovely selection of props.

National Library of Australia
Cataloguing-in-Publication data:

   Passmore, Jacki.
   Curry bible.
   Includes index.
   ISBN 978 0 14 300583 4
   1. Cookery (Curry). I. Title.

   641.6384

penguin.com.au